The
Caring Teacher's
Guide to Discipline

Helping Young Students Learn Self-Control, Responsibility, and Respect

Marilyn E. Gootman

CORWIN PRESS, INC.
A Sage Publications Company
Thousand Oaks, California

For information:

Corwin Press, Inc.
A Sage Publications Company
2455 Teller Road
Thousand Oaks, California 91320
E-mail: order@corwin.sagepub.com

SAGE Publications Ltd.
6 Bonhill Street
London EC2A 4PU
United Kingdom

SAGE Publications India Pvt. Ltd.
M-32 Market
Greater Kailash I
New Delhi 110 048 India

Printed in the United States of America

Library of Congress Cataloging-in-Publication Data

Gootman, Marilyn E., 1944-
    The caring teacher's guide to discipline: helping young students learn
self-control, responsibility, and respect / Marilyn E. Gootman.
        p.   cm.
    Includes bibliographical references and index.
    ISBN 0-8039-6526-5 (cloth: acid-free paper). —
    ISBN 0-8039-6527-3 (pbk.: acid-free paper)
    1. School discipline.   2. Classroom management.   I. Title.
    LB3012.G65   1997
    371.5—dc21   97-4775

This book is printed on acid-free paper.

97   98   99   00   01   02   03   10   9   8   7   6   5   4   3   2   1

Production Editor: Diana Axelsen
Editorial Assistant: Kristen L. Gibson
Typesetter/Designer: Janelle LeMaster
Cover Designer: Marcia R. Finlayson

Contents

Foreword

The *Caring Teacher's Guide to Discipline* has been a delight for me to read. The book is thoughtful, practical, and extremely respectful of teachers and of the multiple judgments needed to educate young children well. Different from other texts on discipline and management, this book avoids jargon as well as polemic and ideological attacks. The reader is assisted to think beyond unilateral authority and hierarchical control. What the reader receives are insights, methods, and ways of helping children to learn self-control so that they may become well-educated, independent, and respectful citizens of a democratic society. Such a goal should be the primary one for all educators who work in public schools.

I've known Marilyn Gootman for many years. I know well her work with children, parents, adults, and schools. She is a wonderful parent, an adept crisis counselor, an insightful supervisor of student teachers, and an experienced collaborator with teachers. What you are about to read is Marilyn herself! She is a passionate and intelligent champion for children and for teachers.

As you begin this book, think about your own practice—how it is and what else it might be. Let Marilyn's words and thoughts provoke and guide your thoughts. At the end, make your own judgments as to how your future interactions with students can help your children live in a respectful, powerful, and pro-democratic learning community. If the goal is utopian, the practices for moving toward a better world are real!

—Carl D. Glickman
University Professor and Chair,
Program for School Improvement
University of Georgia

Acknowledgments

I am extremely fortunate to have a network of supportive loved ones: My husband Elliot is always there for me—encouraging, supporting, and even editing. My children Elissa, Jennifer, and Michael have provided me with much enlightenment about the impact of caring teachers. Their experiences and insights through 45 years of schooling have enriched my knowledge and understanding. Freyda Siegel has helped me understand the voices of both students and teachers. In addition to all the knowledge I have gained from her over the years, I appreciate the countless hours she spent reviewing this manuscript. Gail Karwoski and Carol Kurtz, two very caring friends who also happen to be very caring teachers, have been wonderful sounding boards for my ideas as well as terrific sources of encouragement. My colleague Claire Hamilton has stimulated my thinking about children and their needs. She keeps me on my toes. Finally, it is a privilege to have a secretary like Stephanie Bales, who takes pride in her work and can always be relied on.

To Freyda Siegel—my aunt, my friend, and my mentor.

About the Author

Marilyn E. Gootman, Ed.D., is a member of the faculty of the College of Education at the University of Georgia and a former elementary school teacher. She has a B.A. from Simmons College, an M.A. from Brandeis University, and an Ed.D. from the University of Georgia. She is the author of *When a Friend Dies: A Book for Teens About Grieving and Healing* and *The Loving Parent's Guide to Discipline*. A nationally recognized speaker and writer, she conducts workshops for students, educators, and parents on topics ranging from grief to discipline. Her media appearances include CNN, CBS News, *Sonya Friedman Live*, and *Nightwatch*. For further information on Dr. Gootman's workshops, please contact her at the Department of Elementary Education, University of Georgia, 427 Aderhold Hall, Athens, GA 30602-7122, phone: (706) 542-4244, fax: (706) 542-4277, or e-mail: mgootman@uga.cc.uga.edu.

Introduction

Caring Teachers Can Make a Difference

Children don't care how much we know until they know how much we care.

—Author Unknown

Why do we choose to become teachers? Because we care. We care about children, we care about learning, and we care about the world in which we live. We care enough to dedicate ourselves to a challenging, all-consuming, sometimes unappreciated profession.

Most of us are drawn to teaching because we want to make a difference in the lives of children. However, when reality sets in and we stand alone facing a room full of students, many of whom have personal problems, doubts about our personal effectiveness begin to enter our minds. Just being sincere in our caring about our students simply isn't enough. This book will explore practical strategies for actualizing caring in the classroom so that we can indeed make a

1

difference in the lives of our students while keeping our enthusiasm and idealism intact.

The Caring Teacher's Guide to Discipline is written for teachers and student teachers at all levels of experience as well as for administrators. Experienced teachers will find novel approaches for dealing with the unique needs of the current generation of schoolchildren. Beginning teachers and students preparing to become teachers will find specific discipline strategies as well as a general framework for creating a positive classroom environment. Administrators will find a uniform, practical approach to discipline that can be adapted to meet the unique needs of their school community.

Effective discipline goes hand in hand with effective teaching. Caring Teacher Discipline is composed of two essential facets—how to teach students the skills of appropriate behavior, discussed in Chapters 1 through 5, and how to teach students to avoid inappropriate behavior, discussed in Chapters 6 through 10.

What Is Caring Teacher Discipline?

One of the requirements for our undergraduate education students at the University of Georgia is that they ask their supervising classroom teachers for their discipline approaches, so that our students will be consistent with the classroom teacher. Over the years, the vast majority of teachers have responded to this request with information as to how they set up rules and how they punish students who disobey them. Many have perceived discipline as a control issue: "This is what I do to control the students and get them to do what I want."

Good discipline certainly requires that our students experience the consequences of their misbehavior, but that is only one aspect of the process. The underlying premise of the Caring Teacher Discipline approach is that discipline should help children develop self-control. By focusing on self-control rather than on external control, a tremendous burden is lifted from our shoulders. External control takes its toll on our psyches. It is physically and mentally exhausting to feel as though we constantly have to be on top of children, controlling their actions.

Many teachers consider discipline to be synonymous with punishment. But discipline is not the same as punishment. Punishment focuses only on misbehavior. The goal of Caring Teacher Discipline is to teach children how to do the right thing. This goal is accomplished by setting limits, giving students responsibility, helping them develop confidence in their abilities, and teaching them how to solve problems and make good judgments, as well as by correcting misbehavior. Caring Teacher Discipline aims at taking some of the distastefulness out of discipline. When discipline is viewed only as punishing misbehavior, it can be quite unpleasant and discouraging. Having to punish students is draining because we must assume a negative posture and teach children *not* to do the *wrong* thing. With Caring Teacher Discipline, we can assume a positive posture—teaching children *how* to do the *right* thing.

demonst - rating basic needs.

Caring Teacher Discipline
Saves Time and Reduces Stress

Our goal is to describe a viable, practical approach to discipline. A major concern of teachers is that discipline issues rob them of precious learning time. Some popular discipline programs try to provide teachers with "quick fixes," promising them that they will not have to spend much time on discipline. Unfortunately, with these programs, many teachers find that the same behavior problems resurface within a short period of time and become a constantly nagging issue. The problems let up for short spurts and then reappear. Caring Teacher strategies reduce the amount of time needed to devote to discipline problems by effecting long-term, solid changes in behavior. Once the system is established, and as children learn how to take responsibility for their own behavior, teachers find that the time they must spend on discipline problems diminishes. Yes, the approach does take time and practice initially, but the investment pays off. Teachers who have tried it have found that the recidivism rate for the same infractions is dramatically reduced. They do not have to deal with the same problem from the same child over and over again.

Another major concern with respect to discipline is the amount of stress it places on teachers and students. Caring Teacher strategies focus on cooperation by all of us—teachers, students, and parents working together to solve problems and help children be the best that they can be. The classroom is a caring community; relationships

among the students and between teachers and students are supportive. The positive, constructive attitude is energizing and stress
reducing.

Caring Teacher Discipline:
An Approach for All Students

The first step in the Caring Teacher approach to teaching students
discipline is to create an environment that is conducive to appropriate
behavior. When classroom space and time are clearly organized,
students develop a sense of security, which can have a calming effect
on their behavior. When they know what to expect and when, it is
more likely that they will do the right thing. Suggestions for setting
the stage for appropriate behavior by developing a sense of security in
the classroom are discussed in Chapter 1. Children must also know
what is expected of them, when, and why. Clearly defined rules and
limits are essential. Establishing a system of rules and guidelines is
the focus of Chapter 2.

Students are also more likely to behave appropriately if they have
a strong sense of self-worth. All teachers are familiar with those
children who feel so badly about themselves that they take it out on
us and their classmates. Chapter 3 focuses on strategies for encouraging children and helping them develop positive self-images. Uses
and misuses of rewards and praise, as well as techniques for boosting
students' sense of competence and self-confidence, are explored.

Many discipline problems arise because of poor communication,
either among students or between students and teachers. Chapter 4
presents techniques for opening the lines of communication to solve
some discipline problems, for preventing others from occurring in the
first place, and for developing the classroom into a caring community.

Anger, either ours or our students', presents a tremendous challenge. What do we do when we feel like blowing our stack because
our students' behavior is totally infuriating? (Yes, we all feel this way
at one time or another.) What do we do with raging children who
present a safety risk to us and to their peers if their fury remains
unchecked? Techniques for dealing with anger are presented in Chapter 5.

Even with security, encouragement, and communication skills,
children will still misbehave. Such is human nature. Rather than

being viewed as a failure in the discipline process, every instance of misbehavior can be viewed as an opportunity to teach self-discipline. Chapter 6 discusses what to do after children misbehave. Chapters 7 and 8 present problem solving as a viable tool for dealing with misbehavior. Because the majority of discipline complaints by teachers relate to frustrations over students fighting with each other, Chapter 8 also includes a discussion on how to use problem solving as a model for nonviolent conflict resolution. Chronic, annoying behaviors that crop up in most classrooms at one time or another are discussed in Chapter 9. This chapter explores some of the causes of these behaviors as well as steps that teachers can take to eliminate them.

Caring Teacher Discipline: An Approach for Students With Behavior and Learning Problems

Discipline often poses a great challenge in today's schools because of the pressures society has imposed on individuals and families. The effects of drug abuse, spouse abuse, child abuse and neglect, community and media-generated violence, poverty, and single parenting reverberate in our schools. Many children haul the baggage of dysfunction straight into the classroom and unpack their pain masqueraded in the wraps of misbehavior and underachievement. They push us to our limits and render discipline all-consuming, overshadowing and threatening to academic learning.

These children often present major learning and behavior problems in our classrooms, such as aggression, hyperactivity, spaciness, provocativeness, passivity, hypervigilance, and the inability to concentrate. These problem behaviors are often created by circumstances totally beyond our control. Although we cannot change our students' homes and communities, we can take action within the classroom, and we can ensure that we do not further exacerbate the problems. The Caring Teacher approach to discipline described in Chapters 1 through 9 works with all children, even with those who carry the extra baggage of dysfunction. The difference is in degree, not kind. Chapter 10 discusses how the strategies presented in the previous chapters can be successfully adapted and applied to working with major learning and behavior problems that are the result of trauma.

Certainly, some learning and behavior problems can be attributed to sources other than family dysfunction or trauma, such as physical, neurological, and biochemical disorders. Although these sources will not be directly addressed, the Caring Teacher approach to discipline is also highly effective in these situations. Caring Teacher Discipline provides structure, consistency, empathy, and self-control and can be empowering for students with physical, neurological, or biochemical disorders.

Three Basic Assumptions

The Caring Teacher system is based on three basic assumptions:

Teachers are intelligent professionals who have been trained to use their minds. Some discipline programs try to appeal to teachers by promising that they can provide an instant system where a teacher does not have to take time to think. All infractions can be plugged into the same formula where no judgments, no decisions, and no discussions are necessary.

The concept of instant discipline may sound appealing at first glance. But instant discipline works about as well as instant weight loss programs. They work for a while, but soon we end up at our starting point, and sometimes even worse off, gaining back more weight than was lost. The diet programs that succeed where others fail do so because they are based on the premise that new habits must be slowly formed and reinforced. Behavior must change gradually if it is to remained changed. Anyone who claims to have an all-purpose, instant solution to classroom discipline is selling snake oil. Children just don't work that way. More important, these instant programs are an insult to our intelligence and training. We teachers must use our minds if we are to teach students how to use theirs.

Discipline is a fact of life, a normal part of the process of growing and developing and, therefore, a normal part of the classroom experience. All children begin life not knowing any of the skills of self-control, yet they need to learn them to become independent, responsible, happy, well-adjusted members of society. There is no child who is well disciplined without having been taught what is expected and how to do it. All students misbehave at some time or another. Misbehavior is not by definition a sign of a teaching failure; it's a normal facet of learning and growing. Even model teachers must struggle with issues of discipline at one time or another.

The discipline strategies presented in this book encourage teachers to use their minds, yet they are not excessively time-consuming. They can be easily integrated into the normal functioning of the classroom. Yes, it may take time at first to establish the system, but once students understand the process and learn to control their own behavior, discipline gets easier and easier, taking less and less time. From my own experience and that of countless other teachers, I know that, with practice, this approach takes some of the stress out of teaching and saves precious learning time. In fact, this approach can be infused into daily classroom operations in a nearly seamless fashion so that discipline does not drain away valuable learning time but rather becomes part of the learning process.

Children are not born "bad." All children enter this world innocent, with the potential for goodness. They come into this world totally naked and helpless—physically, socially, and emotionally. It is up to us to steer them in a positive direction. As teachers, we have to teach them the self-control they need to be successful in the world on their own. We have to teach them how to take care of their own needs, how to protect their own health and safety, how to cope with disappointment, how to share, how to express themselves constructively, how to feel good about themselves, and how to respect the needs of others and get along with them.

Unfortunately, for some children, turmoil and mistreatment in their lives have deterred them from actualizing their positive potential. As victims of dysfunctional environments, they develop a negative outer coat. Many problem behaviors are the outward manifestation of trauma experienced by children. Aggressiveness, hurting others without seeming to care, passivity, spaciness, clinginess, and hostility are some of the ways children adapt to the experiential demands of their lives. Although these adaptations may appear maladaptive to the outside observer, often it is these very behaviors that have enabled these children to survive their traumatic experiences. These behaviors reflect a cognitive behavioral style rather than structural damage and, therefore, are potentially remediable (Donovan & McIntyre, 1990). Certainly, we cannot condone these behaviors just because the children have been mistreated. Allowing them leeway because we feel sorry for them or because it's not their fault will only magnify their problems and ours. Later, we will discuss specific strategies for dealing with these problem behaviors and for helping children devise more socially acceptable ways to adapt and overcome their problems. Before we begin, we must acknowledge that these children are victims—they were not born with these negative behaviors—and their internal potential for goodness remains intact. With appropriate encouragement and care, their positive inner core can be brought to the surface.

Locked inside traumatized children are powerful and terrifying beliefs that they are helpless, bad, and at fault (James, 1989). Judith Herman (1992), who has conducted extensive research with abused adults and children, explains that the "profound sense of inner badness becomes the core around which the abused child's identity is formed" (p. 105). These children desperately need adults who can counteract this belief with a message of hope and a faith in their inner goodness. We must convey loudly and clearly that, although some of their behaviors may be unacceptable, they are decent, worthwhile human beings, and that we know they can make it and we will stick by them. We must be reasonable in our expectations and know what is appropriate for the age and development of our students lest we further complicate their problems. Every child, and especially those whose behaviors are manifestations of trauma, must receive genuine, clear messages, such as "I like you," "You are fun," "It's not your fault," "You deserve to be cared for and treated well," and "I will teach you" (James, 1989, p. 13). As James Garbarino, head of the Erikson Institute in Chicago stresses, "the majority of 'at-risk' children in school are developmentally normal—not pathologically disturbed—and have the potential for school success when schools are sensitive to them and their burdens" (Garbarino, Dubrow, Kostelny, & Pardo, 1992, p. 130).

Teachers can make a difference in the lives of children even when these children go home to dysfunction. Considerable research has been conducted concerning what makes children resilient in the face of tremendous odds. Teachers are consistently included in the "protective factors" (individual and environmental characteristics that ameliorate the response to risk factors or stressful life events; see Werner, 1990) that have been isolated by researchers. In fact, "the most powerful influence in overcoming the impact of psychological trauma seems to be the availability of a caregiver who can be blindly trusted when one's own resources are inadequate" (van der Kolk, 1987, p. 32). Study after study confirms that teachers can be this kind of caregiver (Boyer, 1983;

Cicchetti, 1989; Garmezy, 1984; Lynch & Cicchetti, 1992; Masten & Garmezy, 1985; Pederson, Faucher, & Eaton, 1978; Rutter, 1987; Zimrin, 1986).

The most long-term, comprehensive study of high-risk children was conducted by Werner and Smith in Hawaii. The participants in their study were followed periodically from childhood through adulthood. Werner and Smith found that those high-risk children who were resilient all had at least one person who accepted them unconditionally regardless of temperamental idiosyncrasies, physical attractiveness, or intelligence. The authors specify that teachers can play this role and successfully did so for many of their subjects (Werner & Smith, 1992).

Just as we can have a positive impact, so too can we further exacerbate our students' problems. If we are harsh, punitive, and humiliate them in their weakness, or hold them to unreachable standards or to no or minimal standards, then we only make matters worse for both them and us. As their teachers, we often have the power to determine which fork in the road students will take.

Often we become frustrated and discouraged when we see the horror in the lives of some of our most problematic students. We wonder whether our few hours of daily contact can compete with home and community pressures. The evidence is clear. Teachers *can* make a difference in the lives of children even when the rest of these children's lives are in shambles. Caring teachers who believe in the basic goodness of every child can plant a seed of hope and promise inside that will take root and flourish through adulthood despite all other odds.

Catch-22

Unfortunately, some of the children who need our attention and support the most, for whom we can have the greatest positive influence, act so offensively that we may give up on them. These are children who have failed to develop secure attachments to significant adults during their early years (Cicchetti & Barnett, 1991; Crittendon, 1988; Egeland & Stroufe, 1981; Schneider-Rosen, Braunwald, Carlson, & Cicchetti, 1985). Their insecure attachment is manifested in our classroom by behaviors that make it difficult for us to relate to them.

Some children develop insecure attachments because of inconsistent caregiving. At times, they may receive adequate or even effusive care and nurturing although, at other times, their caregiver may be totally unavailable and unapproachable. This unpredictability and ambivalence creates an insecurity in children that often makes them fearfully and hungrily attached, anxiously obedient, and apprehensive lest the caregivers (including the teacher) be unavailable when needed (Bowlby, 1982). Because these children have not developed an inner sense of safety provided by a secure, consistent attachment relationship at a critical period in their lives, they are more dependent on external comfort and solace (Herman, 1992). Anticipating and preventing abandonment preoccupies their every action. Often these children are like clinging vines—they hover by us, we trip over them when we turn around. They are like a bottomless pit; no matter how much attention we give them, it never seems to be enough. They can get on our nerves and try our patience to the utmost.

Other children develop insecure attachments because of detached caregiving. Although their physical needs may or may not be met by their caregivers, the emotional needs of these children are not. Tender touching, love, and genuine interest and care are essential ingredients for a secure attachment relationship. When caregivers are rejecting, detached, or uninterested, children become anxiously attached to others. With no adult to affirm and support them, they often feel worthless. By the time they enter our classrooms, after suffering for years from the excruciating pain of rejection, many have become hostile and rejecting to adults around them as a way to protect themselves from the possibility of further rejection. The risk of continuing to reach out and cling to adults, only to be met with apathy or disinterest, becomes unbearable. Although they crave closeness and love, they feel that seeking it is not worth the pain they will have to endure if they fail. The message of their behavior is, "I'll reject you before you reject me" (Morrow, 1987). Many of us have been deeply hurt by these students at one time or another. After we have extended a hand of friendship and support, and thought we made some sort of connection with them, they suddenly accuse us of unfairness, disparage us, or betray us. These children often respond negatively to anyone who tries to establish a relationship with them. They find solace in being the rejecter/victimizer instead of the rejected/victim. The inner turmoil created by this avoidance while wishing to be near us causes anger to foment inside the child. As their teachers, we suffer the sting of rejection and betrayal, and we become their targets.

Insecure attachment occurs within the normal range of parent-child relationships in approximately 30% of the population (C. E. Hamilton, personal communication, August 22, 1995). It is even more prevalent in the case of abuse and neglect. Abusive parents may be kind and effusively loving with their children at one moment and then full of rage the next. Some beat their children and then hug and kiss them, begging for forgiveness. Because of this extreme parental ambivalence, these children often become clinging vines, thirsting for a positive connection. With neglect, extreme parental apathy is the problem. Neglected children suffer the pain of knowing that no one cares about them, whether it is to feed or clothe them properly, to take them to the doctor when they are sick, or to utter a kind word. Disinterest in and hostility to others is the protective shield that these children erect to protect themselves from the overwhelming sting of apathy-induced rejection.

This behavior, whether it is clinginess or hostility, whether it is in a relatively mild form as the result of "normal" parenting gone amiss, or, in the extreme case, a result of abusive or neglectful "dysfunctional" parenting, can be annoying, to say the least. It makes sense that we find these students difficult to be around and that, because of their behavior, we try to avoid them. These students are also difficult to teach because of their problems. Insecurely attached children often are less ready to learn, have lower cognitive maturity and, consequently, are at greater risk for failure in school (Aber & Allen, 1987; Aber, Allen, Carlson, & Cicchetti, 1989; Cicchetti, 1989). Because they may tend to be less socially competent, these children may fight more with their peers and engage in bullying tactics. However, as we begin to understand the origins of their behavior, we can learn to become more tolerant and to devise ways of providing secure attachment for these children without feeling overwhelmed ourselves.

Once we understand the dynamics of insecure attachment and its manifestations, we are better able to provide those connections that are so essential to the well-being of these children. In addition to the attachments they make with their parents, children develop attachments through ongoing interactions with caregiving adults (Bowlby, 1982). Good intimate relationships with other adults can do much to bolster their self-concept and to make them more effective and more appealing students in our classrooms (Rutter, 1990). In fact, evidence suggests that attachment relations with nonparental care-givers, such as teachers, may have a greater influence on social competence with peers than does maternal attachment. Students who have secure attachment relationships with their teachers seem more socially competent. More social competence means less fighting and bullying (Howes, 1990; Howes & Hamilton, 1992; Oppenheim, Sagi, & Lamb, 1988).

There is hope. Current brain research is providing physical evidence affirming the findings of social scientists. Brain structures concerned with affiliation and bonding are damaged by early social deprivation, but because the number and nature of brain receptors for particular neurotransmitters can continue to change throughout life, it is conceivable that later life experiences can modify earlier depriva-tion changes (van der Kolk, 1987).

By seeing these students through a new lens, we can make our lives more pleasant and their lives more successful. If we realize our potential as teachers—to be an alternative or a compensatory attach-ment figure—then we may be able to build the trust that will help mistreated children negotiate relationships with others and have a successful school experience (Lynch & Cicchetti, 1992).

The key word is *trust*. We teachers can provide "remedial attach-ment" for these students by building their trust in us. For some students, this means finding ways to provide the nurturing and attention that they crave. For younger students, this may mean letting them sit near us when we read a story while, for older students, this may mean engaging them in conversations—in other words, give them "restitutive mothering" (Murphy, 1987). Sometimes it means not giving up on them when they try to push us away. In fact, by rejecting us, they are actually telling us that they care about us but are afraid we will leave them. Simply understanding the dynamics in these situations helps us not to feed the situation and prove their point—that we'll reject them just as everyone else has in the past.

We also build trust by being predictable and dependable. Estab-lishing regular classroom routines can play a vital role (see Chapter 2). Monitoring ourselves so that we do not have sudden outbursts of anger (see Chapter 5) is important for all of our students, but it is critical for children who live in chaotic homes where outbursts are commonplace. If we know we will be absent, we can let them know in advance and reassure them that we will be back. An insecurely attached child may think we'll never come back. It's no wonder that substitutes are given a hard time by these children. They want to get their old teacher back and they'll use any means to accomplish this end. Weekends and vacations may be threatening to these students and can unsettle their behavior. Encouraging them to write a journal or save something to bring back to school when they return reassures them that we have not abandoned them. Rituals, such as reading a special story or shaking hands at the end of the day, also help build security in the child's relationships (Morrow, 1987).

The key lies in interpreting their signals and providing antidotes to their negative attachment experiences. Chapter 10 provides specific guidance to these ends. As teachers, we have the power to extend to them a lifeline of hope and success.

Engaging Parents as Partners in Discipline

Parents are the greatest influence in their children's lives. After all, parents are their children's first and most long-term teachers. Although we are professionally trained teachers for all children, parents are experientially trained teachers for their own children. Doesn't it make sense for parents and teachers to work as partners?

Forming this partnership is sometimes challenged by a tension that often exists between parents and teachers—a rivalry over ownership of the child. On the one hand, as teachers we may feel that because we have objectivity and professional knowledge, we know what's best for the child. On the other hand, parents may feel that because they live with their child day in and day out, they're the ones who know what's best for their child. But as we know, two heads are better than one. By setting aside our rivalries and pooling our knowledge of children in two different contexts, we can accomplish what is truly best for the child.

Building the Partnership

Because many parents are intimidated by our expertise and by the fact that, as teachers, we hold the power of authority, shouldn't we take the first step toward establishing a parent-teacher partnership? We can lead up to a partnership by first putting parents at ease and making them feel welcome in our classrooms. Of course, open houses at the beginning of the year help us to get to know each other. But because the parents of our most challenging students often do not show up on these occasions for whatever reason, why not be creative and try to establish a bond with them in other ways? Here are a few suggestions:

Videotapes: Make videotapes with the students in which the students and the teacher talk to parents and describe what goes on in class. Film regular class activities or perhaps even highlight individual children doing something special.

Newsletters: Prepare chatty weekly newsletters in which teachers and students describe class activities. This keeps parents informed and connected.

Requests for help: Ask parents for help with something that they could do at home. Cutting out shapes, typing a letter, or doing art work, for example, makes parents feel important and needed.

Dialogue journals: Open a dialogue between teachers and parents via a journal that is sent home daily or weekly. The purpose of the journal is to discuss what the child is learning at home and school as well as special home and school events. This is not the place to discuss the child's daily behavior.

Homework: Assign homework where parents become the experts, such as talking about their experiences as a child, their work, or their travel. Or assign homework in which all the parent has to do is listen to the child tell or read a story. This will help draw parents into classroom life.

Class invitations: Invite parents to class celebrations where they can share a special skill or experience with the class, such as ethnic cooking or customs, unusual life experiences, a craft, or information about their profession. This can help forge a strong link with parents and is a wonderful opportunity to provide multicultural experiences for our students.

Partnership When Problems Arise

Once we've established a rapport with parents, it will be much easier to partner with them when discipline problems arise. Putting our heads together with parents when a student has a persistent and/or serious behavior problem is often the best route to a solution. "I'm concerned that Fran has been getting into many fights lately. I wonder if we could get together to see if we can help her with this problem." "I'm concerned" lets a parent know that we care; ". . . to see if we can help her" lets a parent know we are putting the parent on equal footing and want to create a working alliance.

The problem-solving format can guide our conversation (see Chapter 7). As part of the first step in problem solving (i.e., stating the problem), if we listen to parents describe the child's life outside of school, we can gain tremendous insight. Our approach can be that of information gatherer, not advice giver (Morrow, 1987). An underlying assumption when working with parents should be that we don't tell them how to run their households and they don't tell us how to run our classrooms.

When speaking with a parent, perhaps he or she will describe a similar problem at home: "I notice that Fran is fighting with her sister more often." Or perhaps the parent will mention that a relative is ill or that the parents are splitting up. Parents and teachers can brainstorm together to figure out how to help the child overcome his or her problem. Keep in mind that some parents may deny that their child has a problem anyplace other than in the classroom. In that case, we can just focus on the classroom problem. Even if we are quite sure that the parents are denying the truth, debating with them can be counterproductive to establishing a partnership relationship.

Sometimes it may be appropriate to problem solve together with the student as well as with the parents. The key to the success of this process is that all three participants should be on an equal footing, all with the same positive intentions for the child.

At times, we may have to be cautious about how much information we give parents and how we convey this information. Some parents will punish their children at home even though we have already consequented the behavior in school. That's double jeopardy for the child! Some parents will be harsh and punitive if we ask them to help their children with homework. Listening carefully to parents and "sizing them up" will help us to regulate the nature of our partnership so that it works in the best interest of the student. (My book, *The Loving Parent's Guide to Discipline*, published in 1995, adapts the Caring Teacher approach to discipline for parents and can help parents get on the same wavelength as caring teachers.)

Partnership With Abusive or Neglectful Parents

Of course, if we have reasonable cause to suspect abuse or neglect, we are both legally and morally bound to report it. But because many children remain with the abusive or neglectful parent, we still have to work with these parents. Although we may find the actions of such parents reprehensible, isn't it in the best interest of the child for us to establish a positive relationship with their parents? If we let our anger get the best of us, and we treat these parents with hostility, their children may be placed at greater risk. If we assume a nurturing posture, giving these parents encouragement and positive feedback while also giving them specific positive strategies for relating to their children, we may ease the burden on their children. Isolation is a common characteristic of abusive and neglectful parents. That's why keeping in touch with these parents, making them feel welcome in our classrooms, and engaging them in a partnership is so important.

Summary of Main Points

❖ Discipline is a fact of life, a normal part of the process of growing and developing.

❖ Discipline can become part of the learning process rather than a drain on it.

❖ Effective discipline can reduce teacher and student stress.

❖ Discipline is helping our students develop self-control in a way that allows both teachers and students to feel good about themselves.

❖ Discipline is something we do *with* students, not *to* them.

❖ Teachers can enhance the resilience of high-risk children.

❖ Insecurely attached children create discipline problems that can be solved by a caring teacher.

❖ Being a caring teacher requires a blend of attitude and action.

❖ Caring Teacher Discipline strategies are designed to help children become good thinkers and learners as well as good classroom citizens.

❖ Discipline can be enhanced by partnerships between teachers and parents.

1

Setting the Stage for Appropriate Behavior

All the world's a stage and all the men and women merely players.

—William Shakespeare

The world is indeed a stage. When it comes to the lives of our students, we, as teachers, help set the stage so that our students will find it easier to take on the role of a well-behaved person. As stage directors, we can help create a "well-ordered, predictable, physically and psychologically 'safe' environment" (Garbarino et al., 1992, p. 159) that will spur them on to successful future performances.

Recently, one of my colleagues asked me why I don't use the term *classroom management* instead of *discipline*. Her reasoning was that *discipline* sounds like such a harsh word by comparison. "But," I explained, "check your dictionary. Discipline means teaching; there should be nothing harsh about that." Substituting the term *classroom management* for *discipline* contradicts my whole approach (discipline is teaching children self-control, not controlling or managing them).

Nevertheless, classroom management is one facet of effective discipline. Following the stage director analogy, a teacher can manage or direct the logistics of classroom life in a way that makes it convenient for students to behave appropriately. Classroom management, when defined as structuring and organizing classrooms to facilitate appropriate behavior, is the facet of discipline that we will now discuss.

Organization

By organizing space and time for our students, we can take a major step in avoiding discipline hassles.

Space: There's a Place for Everything

In my role as a supervisor of student teachers, I have visited hundreds of classrooms. Sometimes, I feel like I am viewing the aftermath of a tornado—books and papers are scattered around the room, bits of scrap paper randomly dot the floor, students' desks are in disarray. An uneasy tension permeates the air. The chaos seems to put students on edge.

Shelves, bins, file folders, and labels are essential pieces of classroom equipment that can help create a calming security in the classroom. Establishing specific locations and containers for homework, class assignments, pencils, and tools, such as scissors, rulers, and dictionaries, makes it convenient and possible for students to do the right thing. Clear labels help them locate supplies and make it more likely that things will be returned to their proper location.

Then, as stage directors, we can teach our students how to use these various props. With practice and our guidance, students can learn how to be responsible for returning possessions to their proper spot and how to keep the classroom in order. Isn't it delightful when they can be independent because they know where everything is and do not have to keep asking us for assistance? It saves us so much time and energy.

Where we place items is just as important as how we place them. Traffic flow is an important consideration when trying to minimize classroom disruptions. Students should not have to disturb classmates in order to use pencil sharpeners and wastebaskets. Paper and other supplies should be within students' reach if they are allowed to use them when they need to. Homework assignment baskets should be by the door, waiting to be filled as students enter the classroom.

I have found it helpful to reflect on what kinds of activities I would like to promote in my classroom and then organize it accordingly. Seating can be designed to make it more likely that students will do what they are supposed to be doing. For example, tables are ideal for encouraging small-group discussion and for cooperative learning. However, when taking tests, students may find it too tempting to glance at someone else's work if class members are seated at tables. And as any experienced teacher knows, some disruptive behavior can be avoided merely by taking into account personalities and interpersonal chemistry when planning seating arrangements and cooperative learning groups. Certainly, space organization will not solve all discipline problems. It does, however, have significant value as a preventive discipline strategy.

Time

Routines

When we establish daily routines, students have the opportunity to practice appropriate behavior on a daily basis. Routines are important for all students, regardless of their backgrounds. Routines provide security and confidence. When students know what is expected of them and when, they can concentrate their efforts on their work rather than on wondering and trying to figure out what they should be doing. All students benefit from routines, especially those who come from very strict homes where routines are rigid and strictly enforced, and those who come from chaotic home environments where there are no set routines and children never know what is going to happen next. With no classroom routines or structure, children from very strict homes may be terrified. They have not learned how to function on their own. Children from chaotic homes, perhaps with a family history of alcoholism, abuse, neglect, family discord, or sudden overwhelming trauma, such as a death or serious accident, may be hypersensitive to unexpected change. In their homes, they often suffer anxiety from not knowing what will happen next—Will a parent lash out at them? Will someone else die? Will they be fed the next meal? What horror will happen next? Their autonomic nervous systems continue to prepare them for action (van der Kolk, 1987).

Jumpy and on guard, they are on alert for emergencies that no longer exist ("Post-Traumatic Stress: Part I," 1991). Established scheduled and routines in which students know exactly what to expect minimizes their jumpiness. Teachers who provide an organized, predictable environment are particularly effective with these children (Werner & Smith, 1992). The same applies to students with attention deficit disorder (ADD) and attention deficit hyperactivity disorder (ADHD). These students require minimal distractions and a calm, orderly environment. Many lose control when the unexpected happens.

It's up to us to determine the routines that will enhance classroom efficiency and security. We need to consider our preferences, the classroom setup, and our particular students. Many teachers find it helpful to discuss these procedures with students during class meetings as a way to get their input as to how to carry out the procedures, whereas other teachers choose to make these decisions themselves. See pages 23-25 for further discussion on class meetings. The following are some routines or procedures that we can clarify for our students:

- What to do on arrival at school
- Homework: where listed, where handed in
- What to do when the bell rings
- What to do when a pencil breaks
- The format for filling out papers
- Where papers should be turned in
- Where bookbags and other supplies should be placed
- What to do when they have a question
- Bathroom breaks
- Quiet signal
- Going to lunch
- Coming in from recess
- Walking in the hall
- Working in a group
- Dismissal

Because routines may vary from class to class, they must be clearly spelled out for students right from the start. Then, we need to remind students periodically about the procedures. Some classes have a handout or booklet describing procedures to help new students adjust if they join the class later in the year as well as to remind those students who may need a refresher.

Schedules

On one of my frequent visits to a local school, I was shocked to find the usually calm, well-behaved fourth grade wing of the school in an uproar. Students were loud, jumpy, and fighting with each other. They were practically hanging from the light fixtures. I couldn't imagine what in the world was going on (and neither could the teachers) until I heard the triggering stimulus: That morning they were informed that at some undetermined time during the day, they would hear an announcement over the loudspeaker telling them when to go to the cafeteria to rehearse the school play. The uncertainty of not knowing when that voice would boom into their classroom and what they would be missing (perhaps even lunch or recess) triggered a state of anxiety in these children, many of whom had chaotic home lives but usually stable and secure school lives. It didn't matter that the disruption was only to announce a rehearsal. What mattered was that it was unpredictable. The same goes for fire and tornado drills. Some children cannot collect themselves and settle down in the aftermath of such a drill. A biochemical response gets triggered in their bodies. Certainly, we cannot prevent all unexpected events, but if we have a regular routine and a schedule, students will be less likely to go off the deep end when there is an occasional change.

Writing the schedule on the board can be helpful. Whenever possible, on those days when we must vary from our routine, we can let them know in advance. "Today, we'll be eating lunch at 12:00 instead of at 12:30 because . . ." If unexpected change does trigger hyperarousal, it helps to talk the students through it rather than chastise them to settle down. "That was unsettling when the bell rang. It made our bodies jumpy. But now it's over with, and I promise it won't happen again today." Of course, we can only make promises that we can keep. Older children can be helped to process this on a higher level and can engage in discussions about the biochemical and physiological changes that they experience during these times. Using words to help them describe what they are feeling can reduce some of their jumpiness (Herman, 1992).

Although routines and schedules are helpful, rigidity is not. "No, we can't figure out the rest of this problem because it's time for reading" is an unreasonable response. Routines do not have to be etched in stone. We do not want our students to become rigid, inflexible people, nor should we model rigid behaviors. It helps when we are flexible in our routines, revising them for exceptional situations, explaining when and why we are changing them. It also helps to explain why we do not generally change them.

Children from chaotic homes, children from very strict homes, or children with sensorial problems, such as those very sensitive to noise, may be overwhelmed in classrooms that bustle with students involved in a variety of projects on different topics and at different levels. These children may fare best in more structured, organized, and calmer classrooms. Learning styles differ, and so do teaching styles. The ideal is for the person in charge of assigning students to teachers to try to match students with teachers whose style best fit their needs.

Time has a different connotation for children than it does for adults. Children live in the present. They do not have our experience with deadlines or our notion of time as limited. We hurry them, yet they persist in taking their time. When possible, it's helpful to allow our students a little more time than we think they'll need, such as for cleaning up their supplies or preparing to move to the next class. When young children, in particular, are rushed, they tend to feel rejected. Besides, rushing them isn't necessarily going to get them to move any faster.

Transitions

Many children have a hard time going from one activity to another. In fact, one of the most difficult challenges for student teachers is easing the transition from one subject to another. Warning students a few minutes ahead of time helps them get ready and avoids discipline problems that arise when they are not ready. Just as stage managers may announce, "Five minutes to curtain time," we should announce, "You have 5 minutes before recess is over," or "We have to go to lunch in 10 minutes." Then, students who are busy at work can figure out a good stopping point. When students come in from recess, often they are wild. Perhaps they are wound up from running around, maybe they were in a fight, or maybe they were too cold. We can help them refocus their attention and settle down before they are expected to tackle learning. Taking a few deep breaths may help them. I have also found it helpful to be waiting at the door to usher them in—perhaps whispering a reminder about what to do.

As every teacher knows, family dysfunction can cause learning and behavior problems. Children from chaotic homes are often pulled out of the regular classroom for special instructional classes for learning disabilities, reading, behavior disorders, and counseling, among other reasons. Yet, these are the very children who are hypersensitive to changes and transitions. Pulling these students out of their regular classrooms at random times during the day may trigger physiological jumpiness and discipline problems. Blocking out one set time each day for pull-out programs as well as designing inclusion strategies may help prevent these problems.

Another fertile time for discipline problems is that "empty" time for students who finish their work before others. If we don't want them to waste their time and to distract their fellow classmates, then why not anticipate and plan for alternative learning activities or assignments for them? Why not encourage them to keep a book to read for pleasure or a writing folder for journal entries, or arrange for other special learning projects? In the earlier grades, they may be able to go to learning centers in their spare time.

Class Meetings

Starting out the day with a regularly scheduled class meeting can be an excellent vehicle for preventing many discipline problems as well as for solving some of those that do arise. Sitting in a circle facing each other, teacher and students share ideas, solve problems, and plan together. Communication and collaboration among all participants are the goals.

How can we afford to set aside 15 to 30 minutes a few times a week with all the time pressures on us? How can we afford not to? By starting out on a positive note and by engaging students in classroom decision making and problem solving, we make an investment that will bear interest throughout the day. Teachers find that with classroom meetings, fewer problems arise and those that do are solved more quickly and amicably.

The first step is explaining that we are going to establish class meetings because we treasure our students' ideas, and because their participation in decision making is important for the successful functioning of our classroom. Next, we can teach them the mechanics needed to conduct successful class meetings.

Circle Formation. The circle formation facilitates good communication because everyone can see everyone else and no one has a preferential seating position. Convening in a circle can be awkward and clumsy, depending on the room's regular seating arrangement. Why not ask our students to plan the most time-efficient and comfortable way to arrange the circle? We can time them as they try out various arrangements, letting them be as creative as they wish. Once the class chooses the arrangement that they think will work the best and that will take the least time to set up and break down, they can practice setting it up so that little time is wasted convening the circle each day.

Communication Guidelines. Asking students to talk all at once can be an effective entry into a discussion about what guidelines would be helpful so that everyone can be heard. What happened when we all spoke at once? How did it make you feel? Were you able to get your point across? Then, students can design procedures for enabling one person to talk at a time and for giving everyone an opportunity to be heard. Many classes find it helpful to pass around an object, such as a Koush ball, allowing only the person holding the object to speak. Students can pass the ball if they prefer not to speak; then, when the ball comes around to them a second time, they may feel more comfortable and change their minds about speaking. Students will also need our help learning and practicing how to give feedback nonhurtfully. The "I Message" discussed in Chapter 4 can serve as a guide for them.

Setting an Agenda. Everyone in the classroom is allowed to have input into what is discussed during the meeting. Many teachers have found the following basic outline helpful:

• *Positive affirmations:* Why not start out on a positive note where participants compliment each other, acknowledge each other's accomplishments, and express their appreciation of one another? "I appreciate how Alex taught me how to tie yesterday." "I'd like to compliment David on his colorful picture." "I am so happy that Todd is not moving away after all." Learning how to provide positive feedback, as well as how to accept it graciously, takes practice. We can use this opportunity to teach students how to notice the positive and how to provide the kind of meaningful, helpful praise discussed in Chapter 3. Students can also take this time to discuss events in their lives—the birth of a new sibling, the loss of a grandparent, or taking a trip. They can be encouraged to identify with each other's events: "I appreciate how Debbie must feel"; "I remember when my baby sister was born"; or "I remember how sad I was when my grandma died."

• *Discussing problems:* Problems that we or our students have written down and placed in a *problem box* can be discussed by the group. For example, "People aren't sharing balls on the playground"; "Tim keeps humming and it distracts me"; "We don't have enough time at recess"; or "Other teachers have complained that our class is too noisy in the hall." The problem-solving format discussed in Chapter 8 can be used as a guideline for the discussion. If it's a class problem, then the class votes on a solution. If it's an individual problem, then the individual should be allowed to choose a solution from those suggested by the whole group.

• *Making class decisions:* Deciding what would be appropriate class rules and procedures (see Chapter 2), planning a field trip or a class party, deciding which topic to study next in social studies, figuring out how to arrange the classroom, or choosing a community service project for the class to undertake are among the decisions that classes can make as a whole during class meetings (Nelsen, Lott, & Glenn, 1993).

Summary: Organization

Helping our students organize their space and time makes life more pleasant for all of us. When students know where things belong, they are more likely to put them there. When they know what to do, they are more likely to do it. Schedules and routines create a secure environment for all learners but are critical for those who have chaotic home lives. Allowing time for class meetings can set the stage for cooperative classroom behavior.

Modeling

Modeling is another way we direct our students to correct behavior. Children often do as we do, not as we say (Bandura, 1973). Modeling is a terrific tool for teaching our students discipline, but it's also a tricky tool. There are two sides to the coin. Students copy our undesirable behaviors as well as mimic our noble ones.

Doing as We Say

Sometimes we don't realize that we are sending out two conflicting messages to our students when we tell them to act one way but model another way. We may yell at them while exhorting them not to yell. Corporal punishment is another example. Students are paddled for hitting other students. They are hit so that they will learn not to hit. Instead, what they learn is that big people can hit little people, those in power can use physical aggression against the powerless. Actions speak louder than words. When a conflict arises between what we say and what we do, our students will usually copy what we do rather than what we say.

If we want students to hand in assignments on time, then shouldn't we hand them back on time? If we want students to show interest in their work, shouldn't we show interest in ours? If we want students to talk respectfully to us, then shouldn't we talk respectfully to them?

Developing Mutual Respect

Respect is like a boomerang. If we send it out, we will get it back. If we send out disrespect, we'll get that back. Being "dissed" causes kids to lash out at whoever dissed them. Disrespect triggers rage and an uncontrollable urge to send the disrespect right back to where it came from, especially with vulnerable students who are already at risk and who feel hopeless and helpless about their lives. Mutual respect is our goal.

Even when we do send out messages of respect, realistically, we cannot expect that our students will always treat us with respect. Many factors get in the way; they want to look "cool" in front of their friends, they're frustrated and angry, and they lose control. We must confront these situations directly when they occur and nip them in the bud. If, however, we treat our students respectfully, these situations will be few and far between and can be dealt with constructively.

Respect means treating our students as we would want to be treated. We don't like to be yelled at, humiliated, threatened, or spoken to sarcastically, so why should our students? Children are quite fragile and depend on us to help them build up self-confidence and courage to face the world. Respect and self-respect go hand in hand.

Keeping Our Cool

Teaching can certainly be stressful. Some students push us to our limits. Rare is the teacher who hasn't at one time or another felt like Mount Vesuvius about to erupt. But trying our best to keep our cool and learning to channel our anger constructively (see Chapter 5) are critical for teaching our students to do the same.

First, if we model constructive expression of anger, our students are more likely to copy our behavior. For some children, we are the only positive model in their lives. If we don't show them that adults can express angry feelings constructively, then they may *never* see that this is possible.

Second, sudden outbursts can trigger jumpiness and anxiety in all children. For children who come from chaotic homes, our explosions can create that physioneurosis response, which can manifest itself as hyperactive, disruptive, unruly behavior. In addition, children who are unused to outbursts in their homes can become terrified. All children need calm, physically and psychologically safe environments if they are to behave properly and learn.

Summary of Main Points

❖ By organizing space and time for our students, we can avoid some discipline pitfalls.

❖ We can provide props and cues that signal to our students how they should behave, thereby preventing some discipline problems from occurring.

❖ Routines provide security and confidence for all students.

❖ Routines (not rigidity) are critical for facilitating appropriate behavior in students who come from chaotic home environments.

❖ Excitement or unpredictability can trigger a physiological response in child victims of trauma that may make them unfocused and disruptive.

❖ We can eliminate some discipline problems by easing transitions from one activity or subject to another.

❖ Class meetings can help prevent as well as solve discipline problems.

❖ Modeling is a terrific tool for teaching our students discipline.

❖ Respect is like a boomerang. If we send it out, we will get it back.

2

Expectations, Limits, and Rules

Do not make a fence more important than what is fenced in.
—Midrash

The following analogy provides us with a framework for our discussion of expectations and guidelines:

The hikers trudged through the woods to reach a magnificent waterfall. The path up was steep and their hunger and exhaustion were growing, yet they forged ahead, propelled by the exciting prospect of seeing the waterfall. Their anticipation was building as they neared their destination. Up one hill, then another, over a few rocks and slippery spots, and then they were there. They finally arrived only to find a huge barricade blocking most of the view. On it was posted "DANGER, DO NOT PASS BEYOND THIS FENCE." Fuming, they ranted and raved about the park rangers—how could they be so insensitive? Didn't they realize how important the view was to the hikers? One hiker vowed to get back at them and wrote obscene messages all over the barricade. Another, blinded by his fury, decided to scale the 8-foot fence—he was going to see the waterfall regardless. He may have seen the waterfall, but he does not recall anything about the moments before his 20-foot plunge.

A second group of hikers trudged through the woods to another waterfall. Up one hill, then another, over a few rocks and slippery spots, and then they were there—ah, what a view! Straight before them, in all its raw beauty, was a raging waterfall. A fine mist of refreshingly cool water sprayed their faces. But one hiker became panicky. "What if I slip? What if I get too close and fall down the slope?" He cowered near the path, unable to relax until they descended. One of his friends, however, was fascinated by the waterfall. He edged closer and closer to get the best possible view, until . . .

A third group of hikers trudged through the woods to yet another waterfall. They all ran up to the waist-high fence, held the rail, and gazed with awe at this majestic scene. A gentle cool mist sprayed their faces as they relaxed, soaking up the beauty that lay before them.

Learning is our students' waterfall. Our rules are the fences that keep them on the path to enjoying learning, providing our students with safety, security, and the freedom to enjoy and benefit from their education. As teachers, we have the choice whether to build unreasonable barricades, no fence at all, or waist-high fences. Let's examine the effects of these three approaches on student behavior.

Unreasonable Barricades: How Students Respond

"If I don't have very strict rules, my students will walk all over me." "Very strict rules breed character." "This is my classroom and students need to know I'm in charge." These are some teachers' justifications for excessively strict rules. These are the teachers known for running a tight ship. Yes, structure in a classroom is important, but excessive structure and being overly strict often backfires. Here are some ways students respond to unreasonable barricades.

"You Can't Make Me"

As we saw with the hikers, huge barricades that close us off from independence and enjoyment can breed fury, not obedience. When teachers are overly strict, many students seethe inside or rant and rave about their teachers just as the hikers did about the park rangers. Some students seem to go out of their way to break rules if they view them to be excessive and unfair, just as the hiker who climbed the barricade did. They may hurdle the barricades by misbehaving more than they would if the rules were reasonable. Other students get back at their teachers by symbolically writing on the barricades—they are defiant, talk back, and produce work well below their ability. Some deface or destroy school property, or take it out on the teacher's property.

"You Won't Catch Me"

Other students will develop sneaky ways to circumvent the rules. Students who do not understand the reasons for rules and suspect that they exist because teachers don't trust them or because teachers are on a power trip, will figure out clever ways to get around the barricades. For example, if students are never allowed to talk to their peers, they'll develop intricate secret communication systems. If not allowed to get a drink of water when they are thirsty, they may concoct a suddenly urgent bladder or bowel problem. Even when rules are reasonable but are enforced overly rigidly, students often respond with underhandedness.

"Yes, Ma'am"

I cringe every time I see students in a school being chastised and reminded that they must always obey adults and do as they are told without question. Child abusers exploit this admonition and use their authority as an adult to intimidate children and get them to do things the children know they should not be doing. Aren't students who are taught to obey adults, even teachers, without thinking at risk because they may blindly obey any authority figure, even one who may do them harm? "Whatever you say" is their response to all adults. Although feisty students who question our rules and actions may be annoying, these are usually the children who know how to protect themselves from being victims of mistreatment. Obedience is certainly desirable, but blind obedience can have serious negative ramifications for students both in and out of the classroom.

"I'm Afraid"

Some students are so afraid of harsh rules that they cannot concentrate on their school work. They spend so much energy monitoring their every action, trying to do things just right so they won't get in trouble, that their anxiety can block their ability to effectively absorb what they are learning. Their psychic energy is focused on worrying how not to do the wrong thing rather than on thinking about what they are learning.

No Fences: How Students Respond

Setting limits for students is particularly hard for many new teachers. They fear that the students will not like them. But having no rules can be just as harmful as having excessively harsh rules. The following are some responses to classrooms with no rules.

"I Need It Now!"

Every teacher is familiar with the overindulged student whose parents never say no, who set no rules or limits, because they don't want to make their children unhappy or because it's the easy way out, or perhaps because they are just uninterested. Ironically, these children are not happy. These children are impulsive and want everything on the spot, when they want it. They can't handle disappointment. As we know, life is full of restrictions, frustrations, and disappointments. Even if a student pouts or tries to make us feel as though we are mean and unlikable, if we know that we are being fair, then shouldn't we stick to our word? If we do not enforce rules that are important just because we don't want them to get upset, then we are not facilitating cooperative classroom life and we are not preparing our students for the realities of life. Well-adjusted members of society are those who have learned to accept limitations for their own safety as well as for the safety and concern of others so that they can live in harmony with others. In our world, we have to live together in a classroom and rules help us do so peacefully.

"I'm Afraid"

Shouldn't our students experience the security that structure can provide? Imagine the feeling of being at the edge of the waterfall, not knowing how far you could safely venture forward before meeting with disaster! Some students become very timid and fearful in classrooms where expectations are not clearly spelled out. Without the fence that limits provide, they may cower, afraid to take risks, afraid to experience their education to the fullest.

Other students keep searching for our limits. They push and push, getting closer to the edge to find the security of the boundary, not unlike cattle who nuzzle up against the fences when placed in a large pasture. Some students act out, perhaps even becoming destructive to themselves or to others. They are crying for limits, for guidance, for structure—begging for someone to "show me that you care, stop me."

Waist-High Fences: How Students Respond

"I Respect You"

When we establish and explain reasonable rules that respect their dignity and feelings, our students are more likely to respect us. Remember, respect is like a boomerang. If we send it out to our students, it will come back. Here are some common responses to reasonable rules and limitations.

"I Feel Safe"

Even though they won't often admit it, our students need to know that someone cares enough to set down limits so that they feel safe and secure. This is particularly the case for students who do not experience this at home, either because of parental overindulgence, neglect, or harshness.

"I Can Handle It"

As educators, we are preparing our students to function as responsible citizens of our society. Doesn't living in society mean living with rules that are set up for the benefit of all? Doesn't that mean that sometimes we cannot have what we want when we want it or that we cannot do something we would like to do? Students can learn that "I can handle it even if I'm frustrated or disappointed when I have to abide by classroom rules that I do not like."

How to Build Waist-High Fences

Defining Our Expectation

Before we build our waist-high fences, it is important to take a look at what we can reasonably expect out of our educational journey. This chapter is based on the expectation that students can behave in such a way that makes enjoying learning possible and safe for all. Our expectation sets a positive tone and overall direction of the path to learning and, therefore, can become a self-fulfilling prophecy. But we are certainly not so naive as to think that this positive expectation alone will solve all of our discipline problems. Wouldn't that be something! Just expecting the positive is not enough; however, it starts us off on the right foot.

Matching Our Rules to Our Expectation

Rules give students concrete direction to ensure that our expectation becomes a reality. By examining the key phrases in our expectation, we can sharpen our focus as to which rules can serve as waist-high fences to keep our students on the path to learning. These key phrases are "safe," "enjoying learning," and "for all." Only the teacher can determine the specific rules for his or her classroom, but the following are some suggestions for consideration.

"Safe"

Ensuring our students' safety is one of our primary responsibilities as teachers. This includes both physical and psychological safety.

Physical Safety. Physical safety is the most basic of needs that must be met in a classroom. Examples of rules that fall under this category are those that describe what to do in fire and tornado drills, proper playground behavior, proper usage of playground equipment, and proper usage of science equipment. A rule that admonishes students to walk in the classroom and in the halls lest they trip or hurt someone else also falls into this category, as do no smoking on school property and no hitting rules. Unfortunately, in today's violent times, no weapons allowed on school property must be added to the list of rules.

Psychological Safety. Psychological safety is also a very basic need that must be met in a classroom. Guidelines that instruct students to use constructive and nonhurtful language and that forbid name-calling and put-downs fall into this category.

"Enjoying Learning"

Certainly we cannot legislate our students to enjoy learning. Many factors contribute to enjoyable learning, not the least of which is having stimulating, interesting material. But some rules can help facilitate this enjoyment. Protection of property falls into this category. Rules about returning supplies to their proper location, not destroying school property, and asking before borrowing an item that belongs to someone else are some examples.

"For All"

This phrase has two meanings. First, it refers to the fact that a classroom is a community and guidelines may be needed to facilitate living in harmony. Guidelines about one person talking at a time, taking turns, and sharing supplies teach students how to respect the needs of others in their community. Second, it refers to the fact that rules must apply to teachers as well as to students. As teachers, we are members of the classroom community. If we know that our rules are fair, meaningful, and inspire respect for all, then we should be willing to abide by them as well.

Evaluating Our Rules

In designing rules, we must be sure that they C.A.N. be successful: that they are Clear, Appropriate, and Necessary.

Clear. We need to spell out clearly for our students just what it is that we expect of them. If our rule is to use good manners and be respectful, we must clearly specify the behaviors that make up "good manners" and "respect." What is considered to be polite in one culture may be downright rude in another. I have witnessed students who grew up in the north be chastised for not saying "Yes ma'am" to their teachers when they moved south. No one had explained to them that although in the north "Yes ma'am" is considered to be a sarcastic response to someone who is bossing you around, it is a sign of politeness and respect for adults in the south.

Respect is often culturally determined. Looking an adult in the eye is disrespectful in some cultures when not looking an adult in the eye is disrespectful in others. "Be quiet when someone else is talking"; "Keep your hands and your feet to yourself"; "Touch only in kindness and with permission"—these define what students need to do if they are to be respectful of others.

What does talking quietly mean? The decibel levels of "quiet" for most students far exceed a teacher's definition of quiet. Unless we clearly define and explain our terms, students may unknowingly break our rules. We can demonstrate just how softly one should talk to "talk quietly." What does "work cooperatively with others" mean? Many students will need direct instruction in listening, speaking, and sharing to meet this expectation.

Whenever possible, our rules should be stated in the affirmative: "do" rather than "don't." Expressing rules in terms of the behaviors we expect (e.g., walk in the halls) rather than in terms of those we do not want to see (e.g., do not run in the halls) sends students a clear message about how to act. Often, when we tell students "do not," they seem to have selective hearing. They hear the "do" but not the "not" or they may hear only the end of the sentence and not the beginning. What do you think the first thing a young child who is told "Don't put beans in your nose" will do?

Appropriate. It is helpful to examine our rules as to their appropriateness for our particular students' ages and stages of development. Some rules that are necessary in kindergarten may be ridiculous in high school and vice versa. Similarly, some may be appropriate in one culture and not in another. Our classroom rules reflect what we value, both culturally and personally. This is highly evident if we inspect those from other countries. Japanese rules often include bowing to the teacher and cleaning the classroom. Russian rules admonish students not to embarrass their school or class. Classroom rules in many socialist countries stress cooperation among students.

I have been collecting samples of American classroom rules for the past several years. Among the most frequent rules are obey all teachers, follow directions, listen, stay at your desk, raise your hand to speak, keep your voices low, keep your hands and your feet to yourself. A premium seems to be placed on being quiet, keeping to yourself, and doing what you are told to do. As cooperative learning and individual responsibility and decision making are increasingly becoming a part of our educational value system, it is questionable as to whether these rules are still appropriate for today's classrooms.

Necessary. We stop at stop signs because we know they are there to protect us from injury. Even if a police officer is not around, we stop because we understand the importance of stop signs. If stop signs were placed all along a one-way street with no intersections, however, we would be tempted to pass by them without stopping. If our rules represent unreasonable barricades, our students are likely to design clever ways to circumvent or undermine them.

When our classroom rules are limited to those that are necessary for us to meet our expectation that "all students can and will behave in such a way that makes enjoying learning possible and safe for all," students will be more likely to obey them, even when we are not around. When faced with a whole list of rules, many students consider it their personal challenge to find the one rule not on this list. The fewer rules the better. Many teachers have found it helpful to evaluate their rules and procedures by trying to categorize them according to whether they are designed to ensure safety, learning enjoyment, or living in harmony. This provides a framework for examining the value of each rule. Rules that do not fall into any of these categories usually can be discarded. Setting reasonable rules requires thought, understanding, and experimentation. A universal set of rules for all classrooms does not exist. Our classroom guidelines will depend on our values, our school's values, and the needs and circumstances of our own particular classroom.

Selecting Rules

No one best approach exists. Much depends on our own personal teaching style. What matters is that our students are very clear as to what the classroom rules are and what behaviors are required. Also keep in mind that students are much more likely to obey rules, even if some are not to their liking, when they have been included in the discussion rather than when the rules are decreed from above. With this approach, students develop ownership of the rules, and it is not uncommon to hear them remind their classmates who are breaking a rule: "Remember, we discussed that in September."

Approach A. Some teachers choose to select their classroom rules prior to the beginning of the school year and then notify their students about these rules on Day 1. If, at this time, they explain why they need these rules and provide students with explicit instructions as to rule-abiding behaviors, they are more likely to foster compliance.

Approach B. Some teachers choose a constructivist approach instead and allow students to construct their own understanding of why rules are necessary. They then allow students to design rules or guidelines that will help them live cooperatively in the classroom.

Some teachers find it helpful to introduce the topic of rules by reading a story where chaos erupts in a ruleless society and then discussing the ramifications of having no rules or laws. Others have students play a game but do not provide them with the rules of the game. After several frustrating minutes of game playing, students will be ripe for a discussion on the value of rules. Older students might find it insightful to discuss laws and rules from the perspective of world events.

After a discussion of why rules are necessary, students can be invited to suggest what rules they consider to be appropriate for the class. The responses will probably range from the reasonable to the absurd, from allowing one person talking at a time to no homework ever, and that the teacher will provide candy for the class. During this session, we can contribute ideas as well, particularly if we think that the students have left out an important issue (for more information on this brainstorming technique, please see p. 121).

The next step is critical. Together, teacher and students evaluate each of the suggested rules. Rules can be discussed in terms of how they protect people's health and their physical and psychological safety, how they enhance positive relations among students, and how they facilitate successful, enjoyable learning. Some questions to consider are "How important is this rule?" "Is it necessary?" and "How do we benefit from it?"

This discussion will reveal that some suggested rules are unnecessary or inappropriate, whereas others could be beneficial. For example, with a teacher's guidance, students can conclude on their own that they all benefit when only one person talks at a time, and therefore, one person talking at a time would be a valid rule. They would also realize that because eliminating homework might put them at an academic disadvantage down the line and giving them candy would rot their teeth and make them fat, these would not be helpful rules. Brainstorming and evaluating rules can be enlightening for us as teachers. We learn more about what we personally value and more about our students and their ideas.

One of the keys to the success of this approach is that by discussing the pros and cons of each rule, students construct their own understanding of rules and their necessity. When students figure out that behind every classroom and school rule lies a reason that makes sense, they are much more likely to obey our rule than if we simply tell them to do something "because I say so." Sometimes, we may find during the discussion that our students have a valid point and that one of our rules may in fact not be necessary. After one such discussion, a teacher who routinely assigned homework every night agreed that the night after a test, no homework needed to be assigned. Nevertheless, if we still consider a rule to be necessary even though our students disagree with us, it is our prerogative to keep the rule.

This approach requires us to listen to our students and their ideas in a respectful manner. However, listening to them does not mean that we have to agree with them. As teachers, we must have the final say, even if students do not agree with us, and we may have to establish rules that are not of their choosing. The fact that students have had the opportunity to express their opinions makes it more likely that they will be able to accept the rule.

Not every rule can be anticipated in September. The need for new rules may arise as the year progresses. For example, a teacher may initially choose to allow free access to bathrooms only to find that some students are abusing the privilege. In this case, the teacher may decide to institute a rule about bathroom procedures. Also, the older students are, the less time need be devoted to detailed explanations and discussions. Classroom rules can be part of an ongoing discussion throughout the year.

Practicing the Rules

Not every behavior need be written down as an official rule. In fact, some teachers prefer not to put any rules in written form. What matters more than where and how rules are posted is how thoroughly rules and guidelines have been made clear to students. One principal suggests that we should become coaches to our students when it comes to rules. What do effective athletic coaches do? They teach their athletes the rules of the game, help them practice their skills, and then remind them what to do during the game. We teachers must take on the role of coach when it comes to encouraging children to win the learning game.

First, as coaches, we explicitly teach our students the rules of the game and the specific behaviors and strategies needed to obey the rules. Then, we give them opportunities to practice, coaching and encouraging them along the way. Finally, before they enter the real game, we must remind them what is expected of them, giving them tips that will help them live up to our expectations.

As coaches, we must afford our students ample time to practice appropriate behavior. For example, many children will not know how to communicate nonhurtfully with others unless they are allowed to practice doing so through listening and speaking exercises (see Chapter 4). We can't expect all students to automatically behave properly, and practice ensures habit-forming, rule-abiding behavior.

Coaches want their teams to win. That's why before and during the game, they provide their athletes with tips and reminders about what to do. We want our students to win. That's why we, too, should provide our students with tips and reminders about how to behave. "Remember, when we're in the auditorium we . . ." or "When we come in from recess, we . . ." Sometimes students honestly forget rules or get so carried away that they lose sight of them. Reminding students may stop them before they misbehave. Even with all this attention to rules, students will still behave inappropriately—sometimes by mistake and sometimes deliberately. (Consequences for failing to abide by rules will be discussed in Chapter 6.)

About Posting Rules

If we choose to post our rules, or if our school requires teachers to post their classroom rules, it is advisable to post as few rules as possible. Too many rules challenge some children to find and do something forbidden that is not on the list. The Golden Rule, do unto others as you would have others do unto you, has proven to be an effective rule for many teachers. They use this as a framework for discussing specific behaviors implied by this rule.

In my opinion, consequences should not be posted together with rules for two reasons. First, it sets up a negative expectation—here's the rule and here's what I'll do when you break it. When one of my children was in middle school, my husband and I attended the open house at the beginning of the school year. The teacher introduced herself and the subject she was teaching. Then, she proceeded to give a detailed explanation of her discipline system—several rules were posted and alongside them was an equally developed list of consequences. "But," I thought, "what are you doing to teach my child, to spark interest and excitement in learning? Don't tell me what you'll do when my child messes up. Tell me what you'll do to keep my child so busy she won't have time to mess up." Listing rules and consequences together implies that we expect the students not to obey the rules and that we are prepared for this inevitability. Yes, consequences for inappropriate behavior have their place, but not alongside the rules. (Consequences are discussed separately in Chapter 6.)

The second reason why I prefer not to post consequences alongside rules is that what is appropriate as a consequence for one student or situation may not be right for another. *Assertive Discipline* has helped to create a nationwide trend in pairing rules and consequences by advising teachers that rather than thinking about problems as they occur, they can just act with a consequence. Sure, a quick solution would be nice but what an insult to our intelligence! We are professionals who have been trained to make judgments and decisions, on the spot if necessary. Our education enables us to process information so that we do not have to plug in set formulas. Students and circumstances differ. In my opinion, consequences should not be "one size fits all." Exceptions to this would be rules that must be enforced for basic safety. Students do need to know clearly and explicitly the consequence of bringing a weapon to school.

Summary

  Our rules should be designed to keep our classrooms physically and psychologically safe, enjoyable learning environments. The success of our rules and guidelines depends on our investing time and energy teaching, encouraging, reminding, and guiding our students to abide by them.

Summary of Main Points

❖ Students need reasonable limits.

❖ Setting reasonable rules requires thought, understanding, and experimentation.

❖ Classroom rules should be designed to permit safe, enjoyable learning for all.

❖ Classroom rules should be stated clearly.

❖ Students need direct explanations and demonstrations of rule-abiding behavior.

❖ Allowing students a voice in the rule-setting process helps them construct their own understanding of rules and their necessity.

❖ Classroom rules depend on the values of teachers and of the school and on the age, needs, and circumstances of the particular class.

3

Encouragement, Praise, and Rewards

Kind words can be short and easy to speak, but their echoes are truly endless.

—Mother Teresa

Positive feedback can provide children with encouragement that inspires them to behave appropriately. It can give them the courage to put their best foot forward, the courage to assume responsibility for their own actions, and the courage to face life and its challenges.

Expecting the Positive

Isn't it a wonderful feeling when we know that someone has confidence that we'll succeed! "This is challenging, but I think you can handle it," "I expect that you will complete your homework," and "I'm sure you will take care of it" are messages of our confidence in our students' abilities. These are words of encouragement, words that propel the child in the direction of appropriate behavior. Most students want to please us and will try harder to live up to our expectations if they think we believe they can. Expecting that our students will behave properly and will be successful learners makes it more likely that they will do so.

Certainly, just because we have positive expectations does not mean that students will always behave as we wish. No matter how encouraging and positive we are, children will still make mistakes and misbehave. Making mistakes is an essential part of figuring out how to get along in this world. Our positive and appropriate expectations can set them off in the right direction.

Unfortunately, I have witnessed situations where children, for one reason or another (often times race or economic circumstances), are met with negative expectations. They are expected to be poor learners and are expected to be disruptive in class. Not surprisingly, they behave just as the teacher expects! I honestly think their teachers were not consciously aware of these negative messages. We're human, it can happen with us as well, but negative expectations diminish both us and our students. That's why it's helpful to look at each student and ask ourselves, Do I really believe that this student can and will live up to my expectations? How can I let this student know I have confidence in him or her?

If our expectations are realistically high, students will try to live up to them. If our expectations are too low, students will live down to them. That's why having high, but realistic, academic and behavioral expectations for *all* students can be a positive discipline tool.

Praising

Every single person on this earth, and especially a child, needs praise at some point. When we hear good things about ourselves, isn't it encouraging? It makes us feel good and motivates us to succeed and act appropriately. Yes, praise can encourage our students and give them the lift that inspires them. But not all praise is encouraging. In fact, some praise is downright discouraging and may even push children toward misbehavior. The difference between encouraging and discouraging praise lies in whether its origin is in controlling or noncontrolling (Deci & Flaste, 1995). Praise given to control another person's behavior is devaluing to the recipient because he or she knows it is not sincere and is designed to manipulate. How do you feel when someone tells you how great you look just before they ask you for a favor? How must a student feel when you say that he or she is sitting down nicely only because you want the rest of the students to sit down?

It's awfully tempting to use praise to control children's behavior. With so many pressures placed on teachers today, from overcrowded classrooms, increasing numbers of students with behavior and learning problems, and demands to raise test scores, it is no wonder that we feel out of control and seek approaches that will quickly help us regain a sense of control. Controlling others is often a knee-jerk reaction to feeling stress (Deci & Flaste, 1995). Many times, we grasp at praise as a tool to help us maintain discipline and control. When used as a weapon of control, however, this technique can backfire. There is mounting research evidence that control can exacerbate rather than ameliorate our discipline problems (Deci & Flaste, 1995). Power methods can lead to resistance, rebellion, and lying (Gordon, 1989).

Guidelines for Giving Praise

How can teachers develop the skill of providing appropriate encouraging praise to our students, praise that can give them fuel to continue along a successful path? How can we be sure that our students interpret the praise in the right way? Here are some basic guidelines that can help ensure that our praise achieves its intended purpose.

Remember to Acknowledge the Positive to a Child Who Needs It, Be It Ever So Slight

"Steve, I noticed you sharing the ball with John and playing so cooperatively with him since we came out 5 minutes ago." Playing on the playground for 5 minutes without getting into a fight might not seem like a big deal for most children, but for the child who is constantly picking at and fighting with others, those 5 minutes are gold. Acknowledging that accomplishment can encourage the student to continue along a positive path. If we don't acknowledge it, we will probably lose the window of opportunity to give them encouraging praise because children like that can be "good" only for so long.

Derek rarely brought back homework assignments. One day, he brought in a partially completed assignment. His teacher could have scolded him for not completing the assignment but instead commented on the fine quality of the work completed. The next day, Derek brought in his assignment totally completed. Praise for the incomplete assignment spurred him on to completing more work.

Sometimes it's easy to forget to notice what our students have done right, especially with the troublemakers. We zero in on what must be corrected. But students need to know what they are doing right as well as what mistakes they make. When they are changing their behavior, why not tell them how well they are doing, even if they improved just a little? With some troublesome students, it's a challenge to focus on the positive, and we have to deliberately ask ourselves, "What has he done today that's right?" Their misbehavior glares out at us; sometimes they intentionally do whatever they can to get on our nerves. Nevertheless, by seeking out the positive in them and genuinely praising them for progress, we can encourage them to be more responsible. By our believing in them and commenting on their positive behaviors, they will be encouraged.

"Catch a child being good" has become widely dispensed advice to teachers and parents. Some schools even give well-behaved children T-shirts that say "caught being good." Catching a child being good is not quite the same as the Caring Teacher concept of praising by noticing the positive, for at least three reasons:

1. Using the word *catch* implies that we have to search hard and perhaps do not expect to find the behavior. Caring teachers expect that their students will do the right thing.

2. Using the word *catch* draws children into a game with us of acting appropriately only when they think we'll notice them doing so. While visiting a school with a catch-a-child-being-good policy where students "caught" are praised over the loud-speaker, I witnessed the following two scenes. A child was walking in the hall and saw a piece of paper on the floor. He looked around, saw the teacher from next door, and then very dramatically picked up the piece of paper and deposited it in the

wastebasket near the teacher. A few days later, the same child walked down the hall and saw a gum wrapper on the floor. He looked around and saw no one (he thought I was heavily engrossed in a book), so he stepped over the wrapper and proceeded on his way. If he wouldn't be caught doing good, why bother? Caring Teacher Discipline's aim is to teach students to do the right thing even when we're not looking.

3. "Catching" children is unrealistic. There's no way that we can always catch children when they're being "good." With Caring Teacher Discipline, we don't have the burden of always having to be on the lookout.

Mean What You Say

Did you ever run to the store for a last-minute item, feeling bedraggled and unkempt, hoping no one would see you? Then, just as you are about to slink out the door, someone you haven't seen for a while calls out your name. Hesitantly, you approach and the person exclaims how marvelous you look. What did you think? Chances are, one of these thoughts passed through your mind: "Wow, I *really* must have looked horrible before"; or "What a phony person—I can't believe a thing this person says"; or "Why is she saying this? Does she want something from me?"

How does it feel when someone tells you that you did a great job when you know that you didn't? Discouraged from improving because minimal effort seems to satisfy that person? Embarrassed or down on yourself because you know the person felt sorry for you and therefore gave you a compliment? Mistrustful of that person because he or she was dishonest? Disrespectful of that person's judgment? Wondering what the person wants from you?

We educators have been bombarded by "experts" cautioning us to be positive with our students and to praise them whenever possible. We are told "Praise them and they'll obey you." "Praise them and they'll have high self-esteem." "Praise them and they'll be more successful students," as if praise were the key to teaching success. Praise given just for the sake of praise can do more harm than good. Dishonest praise discourages children as well as adults and can be damaging to their self-esteem. The intentions of the praiser do not matter. What matters is how the child feels as a result of the praise.

If the child figures out that the praiser is just trying to make him or her feel good (and children are *very* perceptive), then he or she may feel worse. "Gee, I must be pretty pathetic if you feel you have to praise me to make me feel good." If it's praise for mediocrity, with the hope that the praise will motivate them to do better, children often end up feeling worse than before and distrust teachers, parents, and other adults even when they praise them for real. Before we praise a student, we should ask ourselves "Do I really mean it?" and if we don't mean it, let's not say it.

Focus on the Deed, Not the Doer

When praising, it's best to stick to a single issue and not cover the child's whole personality in one fell swoop. Stay focused on the deed, on what the child did, rather than on the doer—namely, the child. When Derek hands in a neatly written paper, say, "This paper is very neat," rather than "You're such a good student for handing in this neat paper." When a student gets 100 on a test, say, "That's a nice accomplishment. You studied and learned all the spelling words," rather than "You're so smart." When a student writes an interesting story, say, "That story kept me spellbound," rather than "You're such a terrific writer."

Vague praise that focuses on the child's whole personality rather on the deed does not encourage students because they can't learn from it (Levinson, 1992). "You're such a good writer" gives a student far less information than "Your use of descriptive adjectives helps paint a clear picture of the scene in my mind." Students are encouraged by praise that lets them know what specifically they are doing right.

Turn the Pride Back to the Child Whenever Possible

Alex has been struggling with multiplication when suddenly it clicks. He can now master the times tables. When he receives his first 100 on the test, it may be tempting to write "I'm so proud of you!" across the top of the paper because we are proud of him, and rightfully so. But by doing so, we are focusing on ourselves—on our pride. Wouldn't Alex feel even better if our praise focused on him instead? "You must feel so good. You worked so hard!" or "Quite an accomplishment!" "That's an unusual/interesting way of tackling that!" "This is quite an improvement," and "It looks like you put a lot of work into this" are words that bring students more encouragement than "I'm so proud of you."

When we focus on our pride, we are using praise as a tool for controlling students' behavior, and they become dependent on us. "Do this, and I'll be proud of you." Students get the message that if they conform and do well, they will earn the praise and acceptance of the teacher (not that this is a negative, but it should not be their prime motivation). The praise serves as a reward rather than as a genuine expression of delight in accomplishment. By contrast, turning the pride back to the student is a way to encourage the child to praise and feel good about him- or herself.

Stick to One Person and Avoid Manipulative Setups

"I like the way Katie is sitting so quietly." "I like the way Ted is busy doing his work." "I like the way . . ." has become a very popular discipline tool in many schools. The teacher praises one child to get the other children to follow suit. Does it work? It all depends on how we interpret the word *work*. Yes, younger students usually hustle to copy each other's behavior. So it works for the moment. But if "working" means changing students' behavior in the long run and teaching self-control while maintaining a positive relationship with them, it is doubtful that this approach will work. Certainly, we teachers have the best of intentions in using this technique, but I think we have been misled by the "experts" who tout this approach and make us feel like this is the be-all and end-all to positive discipline. They have neglected to warn us that this form of manipulative praise has several built-in pitfalls.

Focus on the Teacher. This praise is mainly focused on being noticed by the teacher, on the child's trying to please the teacher, rather than on doing what is right because it is the right thing to do. Consequently, this kind of praise is actually a tool to externally control behavior and does not teach the child how to control his or her own behavior.

One teacher recalled the personal affront she experienced when, after she had just told a student that she liked the way she was sitting so quietly, the student spit at one of her classmates a few minutes later. "Imagine that, spitting at someone after I just gave her a compliment," she fumed, furious because the child did not appreciate her compliment. The teacher thought that passing a compliment to her would change the child's overall aggressive behavior. Of course, it takes much more than that. Compliments such as that can trigger immediate conformity, but there is precious little crossover into other behaviors.

Short-Term Changes. The behavior changes from this kind of praise are usually remarkably short-lived. They may last for that lesson but seldom beyond. If it worked in the long run, then "I like the way . . ." would not be echoed throughout some classrooms hundreds of times every day.

Personal Rejection. Many children hear the "I like" and interpret it as a personal rejection. "The teacher likes Katie. The teacher likes Ted." From this they conclude, "The teacher doesn't like me." It matters little that this is not our intent—what matters are the translations that children make.

Resentment. The one who was praised may feel used by the teacher, and the other children often feel resentful. We can just imagine what might be going through the other students' minds: "Boy, that Katie, what a Goody Two Shoes. I can hardly wait to get back at her"; "Why does she always compliment the bad kids when they do one little thing right? How about me? She never notices me"; or "Ted thinks he's perfect. He's just the teacher's pet." Shouldn't we be sensitive to the effect on the group dynamics of the classroom with any discipline approach we adopt?

Stick to One Person and Avoid Comparisons

Any kind of praise that involves comparisons to others, not just the "I like" form, can discourage children. "You're the best math student in our class." Suppose that later on, this same student has trouble in math? "I wish I could depend on your classmates to do their work the way you do." Suppose that same student forgets to do an assignment the next day? How can they ever live up to all this praise? In fact, such comparative praise can become quite a burden to students.

What happens when a child is praised at another's expense? "You are a much better student than your sister." "Unlike your friend Andrew, you finished all your work on time." Comparative praise such as this is a put-down and only makes students resentful of each other. Often, the praised student feels guilty and uncomfortable ("Gee, I know my sister really worked hard") or, worse, gloats about it ("Ha, ha, I'm better than you are!"). A good rule of thumb is, give praise without comparisons.

Cool It

Just as flies can drown in too much honey, children can drown in too much praise. Too much of anything is not good. Too much praise can be just as harmful to a child's budding sense of confidence as not enough praise.

Sometimes, when we praise children too much, we are setting them up for disappointment. They develop unrealistic expectations for themselves that are unlikely to be met. Caroline was at the top of her class. She received numerous "best student awards" and her teacher raved about her abilities. Whenever another student was confused, she'd suggest "Ask Caroline—she knows it all." Caroline's parents decided to transfer her to a high-powered private school. Suddenly, Caroline was no longer being singled out for her high achievement. In fact, her abilities lay right in the middle of those of her classmates. Caroline began to feel insecure. She felt inadequate— she was letting herself and her teachers down.

When we praise too much, we can create "praise junkies," students who cannot function without massive doses of praise. Self-control is beyond their realm; they are controlled by praise. Praise "fixes" motivate them to succeed or to conform. They often perform only when someone notices them. If the report won't be graded, they'll put in minimal effort. If no one is around to compliment them on their neatness, they'll throw trash on the ground.

Some children become so dependent on praise that they feel they are unworthy if they have not been praised for something they do. "Nobody said anything about my story, so I guess it's not very good." "The teacher didn't tell me my picture was nice, so I guess it isn't very good." We can't possibly comment on every piece of work for every child—and we shouldn't have to. But those children who are used to being praised all the time interpret the absence of praise as a negative statement.

Although excessive praise can generate disappointment for some students, it can make others frightened at the prospect of not being able to live up to expectations. "How will I ever be able to keep this up?" "What if I mess up? Then what will my teacher think of me?" It's important that we be realistic in our praise. If everything is *great*, *super*, and *marvelous*, these words lose their meaning as superlatives. Praise should be gauged to fit the accomplishment (Seligman, 1995). And if we praise students just to make them feel better, they'll see right through us and may become discouraged, "Boy, I must be in a bad way if he's praising me for nothing." Even with the caveats we've discussed, we should not hesitate to praise our students. Honest, sincere praise that is not manipulative and stays focused on both the issue and the child can be a tremendous source of encouragement for our students to behave appropriately.

The Artful Critique

One of my student teachers was teaching a math lesson on fractions to her class. She asked a child which of two fractions was larger. The child gave the wrong answer. The student teacher looked at him, smiled, said "Okay," and then went on to ask the same question to another child. "Why didn't you let him know his answer was wrong?" I asked later. "Because I didn't want to discourage him," she replied. She wanted him to feel good about himself, so she didn't tell him his answer was wrong! She smiled and said "Okay" because she thought she always had to be positive with students!

Certainly our students need positive feedback. Hearing good things about themselves is a source of encouragement, but only if the feedback is honest and realistic. Shouldn't we also let students know when they are wrong lest they fail to learn how to attain high standards? The "feel-good" movement that has swept our schools places such an emphasis on being positive that it has made many of us feel guilty if we give corrective feedback to students, and it has created a generation of students who do not know how to accept constructive criticism. Rather than embracing feedback as an opportunity to grow, many students take corrective feedback as a personal rejection and affront.

Some teachers fear that they may be wounding their students' self-esteem by giving constructive criticism. The truth is that self-esteem will ultimately be hurt by the incompetence that results from not correcting one's own mistakes. Self-esteem will be enhanced by the competence achieved from the hard work of correcting one's own mistakes.

"Now that's stupid" is cruel and destructive feedback. But "That's not the answer. Let's see how you came to that" or "I see why you might have thought that, but it's not quite right" kindly lets a child know he or she has made a mistake while helping him or her save face. Self-esteem is hurt by a false sense of correctness, but it is enhanced by learning how to correct one's own mistakes. Our students can grow if we provide them with an "artful critique" (Levinson, 1992). An artful critique is constructive feedback that is specific, offers a solution, and is sensitive. The artful critique enables students to develop a hopeful, optimistic outlook. They learn that they can do something about their setbacks and that it is within their power to make improvements.

This strategy of praising and rewarding students only to make them feel good about themselves has been a major contributing factor to the problem of grade inflation. After all, poor grades might discourage students who have been working hard. This problem has extended up to the university level. "But I worked so hard, I deserve a better grade" echoes through the halls of academia. Many students now feel they are entitled to good grades, if not for the quality of their work, then for the quantity of time they devoted to it. They expect to be rewarded for their efforts. For many, that's what they've been used to throughout their schooling.

But this is a very dangerous tactic. How would you like to drive over a bridge built by an engineer whose teachers never gave him or her constructive criticism? Or how would you like to have heart surgery performed on you by a surgeon whose teachers never used the artful critique?

Rewarding

In some cases, rewards can be an effective tool for encouraging students to behave appropriately. Two kinds of reward strategies exist: planned and spontaneous. Planned rewards are promised ahead of time to students on the condition that they do what they are asked. The reward is contingent on desired behavior. Children earn prizes, food, and free time for good behavior. Typically, points, checks, or stars are collected throughout the week and are then translated into some sort of reward to be given to deserving students at the end of the week. "Everyone received three smiley faces this week so we'll have a popcorn party today." Spontaneous rewards are unexpected and come after the behavior; no conditions for the reward have been set ahead of time and the student does not know in advance that it will be received. "We worked hard all this week, let's have a popcorn party."

Planned Rewards

Planned rewards are extremely popular because many teachers feel that they are easy to use, don't take much time, give immediate results, and appear to be positive. Before we look at the positive aspects of planned rewards, let's first examine a few caveats.

Recently, I visited a classroom where those children who had accumulated a specific number of stars would earn the right to go on a field trip on Friday. By midweek, some students had already earned their stars. They lost their incentive to keep up the good behavior and began misbehaving and getting into trouble. Only when the teacher threatened to take away the stars did they shape up. By Thursday, there were a couple of children who had so few stars that it was virtually impossible for them to accumulate enough for the field trip the next day—they totally gave up—they did what they pleased because they knew the trip was hopeless anyway.

Planned reward systems can inhibit students' ability to develop responsibility for their own behavior. They rely on the control of the reward rather than on their own internal controls to do what's right. Research has found that rewards reduce student interest in performing the behaviors for their own sake (Sternberg, 1990). Yes, the control factor is sometimes reassuring to us, especially when we feel overwhelmed with our responsibilities. But is it worth the long-term price of having students who do the right thing only when we are there to reward them for it? After all, "*Self*-motivation rather than external motivation, is at the heart of creativity, responsibility, healthy behavior and lasting change" (Deci & Flaste, 1995, p. 9).

When my son was in second grade, an excellent teacher, very well meaning, promised her students a Classic Coca Cola for every classic book they read. Eager for the refreshing taste of a Coke, Mike took out *Kim* by Rudyard Kipling from the library and began to read it. The rest of us in the family realized that this book was far beyond his reading level, but he kept turning page after page. When asked whether Kim was a male or female, he wasn't sure. "Then how can you say you read this book?" we all chimed in. "Well, I did all the words!" he responded. Sure enough, he did "do the words"; he ran his finger over every single word in the book. Children can be very clever in finding the shortest path to a reward. Yes, when we reward, we increase the likelihood that they will do something, but we change the way they do it. When it comes to discipline, we can pay a big price when children seek the quickest path to the reward but don't internalize appropriate behavior.

Research evidence suggesting that reward systems are counterproductive is astonishingly comprehensive (for a thorough discussion of this research, see Kohn, 1993). When students are externally motivated to behave appropriately, their ability to internalize this behavior is seriously compromised. They lose any incentive to continue acting in the desired way when there is no goody to be gained (Kohn, 1991).

Classroom discipline reward systems are based on behavior modification theory. According to this theory, rewards should be gradually removed so that, eventually, the recipient will no longer need the reward to maintain the appropriate behavior. Unfortunately, on numerous occasions, I have witnessed just the opposite. "I worked really hard on that assignment, can I have two smiley faces?" "We were really quiet with the substitute, shouldn't we get three checks?" I visited one classroom where it took the teacher 45 minutes on a Friday to tally the hundreds of checks her students had received during the week. Rewards can become addictive. Just as addicts need to increase their dosages to get the same high, so, too, do many students need more and bigger rewards to get them to behave appropriately. "Give me more, more, more" often becomes the theme song of students when planned rewards are used as the primary approach to discipline. "The more rewards are used, the more they seem to be needed" (Kohn, 1993, p. 17).

The more we use rewards, the less they work because they become less meaningful to our students. If not "Give me more," then "Who cares?" eventually becomes a common response to the promise of a reward. Too much of anything is not good. No matter how much we like ice cream, if we have it several times a day, every single day, we will probably get tired of it.

Planned rewards often result in children taking on a very selfish approach of "I'll do it only if it benefits me." A well-loved school counselor described the following incident to me. She was carrying a heavy load of books and needed help opening a door. A student who was on a strict behavior modification reward program with a local psychologist was walking the other way. She asked him to open the door, but he shrugged and said he was not heading that way. There was no reward in it for him, no external incentive for him to be kind to another person.

Too many rewards end up robbing children of the desire to do something because they know inside that it's the right thing to do. Some excessively rewarded children are nice to people only when they think those people can help them, they may keep their own space clean but have no respect for public places, and they read a book only if they are getting school credit for it.

Behavior modification theory also suggests that we be consistent in rewarding appropriate behavior when it occurs, yet this is impossible in a classroom. We can't possibly notice every time each child does the right thing. A teacher wrote the names of the previous day's hard workers on the board each morning. One morning a little girl came in, looked at the list, didn't see her name, and began fuming and pouting: "I worked hard yesterday, why isn't my name up there?" She didn't recover for the rest of the day.

And let us remember, rewards for some mean punishment for others. The child who does not receive the reward considers him- or herself punished. In fact, the use of rewards and punishments in classrooms has been found to be highly correlated—a teacher who uses rewards is more likely to use punishments as well (Newby, 1991). From my own personal experience, I have noticed that to be the case. Classrooms that have detailed reward systems usually have detailed punishment or consequence systems as well. (Certainly, I do not mean to imply that consequences are not appropriate—I will discuss them later in Chapter 6. Here I am referring to punitive consequences.)

Let us also keep in mind what rewards do to group dynamics. One of my daughters was in a class where students earned a bag of popcorn if they behaved appropriately all week. One Friday, she came home quite distressed. She earned her popcorn, but the little boy next to her didn't. In fact, he never earned popcorn. She perceived him as really trying to behave but just messing up. She felt so bad for him that she sneaked and shared some of her popcorn with him. The end result was that she worried about what might happen to her and felt resentment toward her teacher.

On the other hand, there are some children who gloat when they win the popcorn or the prize. They lord it over those who remain unrewarded. What does this do to peaceful coexistence in the classroom? Any time we set up a system where there are winners and losers, when some children get the goodies and others must stand by and watch, we are endangering the classroom climate. Yes, "that's life." There will always be winners and losers in life. But the best way we can fortify our students to be able to cope with life is not by giving them practice in losing but by building up their self-confidence, skills, and ability to work well with others.

We must also consider the fact that, often, it is the same children who miss out on the rewards. Some students never seem to get the popcorn, the extra recess, or the prizes. If that's the case, then the system clearly is not working; for them, the rewards are not motivating. Furthermore, they are usually the very children whom we are targeting with our reward systems. Most students in our classes would behave appropriately even without the promise of a reward system in the first place. So if rewards don't work for the major problem misbehavers whom we are targeting, why bother using them?

With all these caveats aside, never say never. Despite all these reservations, planned rewards can have their place in teaching children discipline. Planned rewards are most effective when they are used occasionally for a specific behavior problem—for example, bad habits, such as thumb sucking or speaking out—that can't seem to be solved any other way (see Chapter 7 for suggestions as to how to first try problem solving to tackle the problem). For straightforward tasks, rewards can help people perform better (Amabile, 1989). The key to this approach is to eventually get the student to behave appropriately automatically, without needing a reward. At first, every time the child behaves appropriately, that child must be consistently rewarded. After a period of rewarding every single time the child behaves appropriately, the reward should be given less frequently, such as perhaps after a week of appropriate behavior and then later after a month, until gradually the rewards become farther and farther apart, and the child behaves appropriately automatically without thought of a reward.

Mrs. H. gave Jamie a sticker each day he didn't hum aloud in class. After Jamie started getting stickers every day in a row for two weeks, Mrs. H promised him a fancy pencil with music notes on it if he consistently didn't hum for a week. After giving Jamie three pencils, Mrs. H. promised him a special pencil case if he didn't hum for a month. By the end, Jamie was no longer humming aloud without any promise of reward.

Most teachers find charts helpful when they use a reward system. On a chart they keep a tally and record each time the child exhibits the behavior they are trying to encourage or doesn't exhibit the behavior they are trying to discourage. The child may get a check or a sticker on the chart. After so many checks or stickers, the child receives a reward. The visual chart helps the child keep track of his or her progress. The child may consider the sticker itself to be a reward. Teachers have found this approach, when used *sparingly*, to be helpful in making children conscious of their behavior and thus extinguishing annoying behaviors that have become unconscious habits, such as making extraneous noises or tapping on desks. Teachers have also found this approach successful with special needs students.

A note of caution: Some rewards have problems built into them. Using money as a reward teaches children that they can try to pay people to get them to do what they want them to do. "I'll give you 5 dollars to write the paper for me." Using food can create eating problems, especially with sweets. "Don't cry, have a cookie" has taught many young children to resort to food to solve their problems, only to develop eating disorders as adults. It's best to give a reward that is logically related to what we want the student to do and that will make sense to the student.

The kind of rewards we give our students sends a message about what we value. We spend hours of classroom time teaching students about proper nutrition, the food pyramid, and the need to avoid excessive sweets and fats. Isn't it hypocritical if we then turn around and give them candy and other sweets when they behave appropriately in the classroom? What must children conclude if we are willing to give them something that we have labeled unhealthy for them just to get them to obey us? One teacher I know allows the children who have earned enough checks at the end of the week to bring in a junk food snack on Monday. The rest of the class can bring a snack, but it must be healthy. What do students learn from this? If homework is important, then why should no homework be a reward? Either homework serves an educational purpose or it doesn't. If it doesn't, why have it? If it does, then the child who earns a night of no homework is losing out.

I have visited classrooms where art projects, reading to the class, and field trips are listed as rewards for good behavior. If, instead of using them as rewards, teachers incorporated these activities into their teaching, they would find that the students would be more motivated to learn and less likely to misbehave. There is no substitute for developmentally appropriate, hands-on, stimulating learning when it comes to preventing discipline problems.

If you do decide that a reward program might be helpful in a particular situation, then try to choose a reward that makes sense to your students and is logically connected to the behavior that you are trying to encourage. For a child who yells out jokes, if he saves them up and stays quiet, then he will be given a few minutes at the end of the day to tell jokes to the whole class while they're getting ready to go home. He gets the recognition he needs, and we get the peace and quiet during teaching time. Some deeds have their own reward built into them. "When you finish this assignment, you can choose a book to read." "Friday afternoon is catch-up time. If you've completed all your work and you have no catching up to do, you can choose from among these games." "If you clean your desk, you will be able to find what you need." "If you read, you will enter a world of excitement and adventure" (as opposed to a currently popular program where, if you read, you receive pizza. Many teachers have found students picking short books, reading them with precious little comprehension just to get the pizza. In essence, they merely "do the words" but fail to find delight in the pleasures reading can bring us). Nontangible rewards, such as allowing children to share their work with the class, help students motivate themselves. Many students delight in the attention they receive when they are chosen to read their work in the "author's chair" or to place their work of art on display.

Spontaneous Rewards

"We've worked so hard today, let's take an extra recess." "It sure was stressful taking all those achievement tests. Let's watch a movie to chill out." "We've had a great week. Let's have a popcorn party today." These are spontaneous rewards. These rewards are given after the fact without the terms for the reward being set ahead of time. These rewards are not meant to control children's behavior but rather to celebrate their accomplishments. The element of surprise makes these rewards more meaningful.

Rather than promising our students rewards ahead of time to get them to do what we want, we can rejoice with them when they succeed. Students receive the message that we genuinely care about them, that we appreciate their effort, and that we are sharing with them rather than ruling over them. Celebrations over accomplishments create a strong bond between us and our students.

Our American culture places far too much emphasis on competition and winning. Classroom reward systems often have a very negative impact on the classroom culture. Students are pitted against each other, labeled winners and losers, rather than working together cooperatively. Jealousy, vindictiveness, and resentment erupt when classmates vie with each other for rewards. Students aren't as willing to help each other out. "What's in it for me?" is their biggest concern. One teacher recalled how, when she was a student, her class had weekly spelling bees. When she missed a word, she returned to her seat and prayed that other children would make mistakes also. When we have general classroom celebrations over accomplishments, we inspire a cooperative atmosphere. "Blake brought in his homework all week. Thanks Ricardo and Duane for calling and reminding him. Let's all have popcorn today to celebrate Blake's accomplishment." Students then feel that everyone is working together, students and teachers, rather than feeling as though we teachers are working against them or trying to control them. This is a much more positive arena in which discipline can take place.

Summary: Rewards

Teachers should ask themselves some guiding questions to decide how to use rewards as tools of encouragement:

- Does this reward make sense to the student? Is it related to what I want the student to do?
- What message am I sending to the student by offering this reward? "I care about you. I want to help you by giving you an incentive" or "I'll have to bribe you because I'm desperate."
- Does this reward encourage long-term behavior change?
- Will my student eventually be able to behave appropriately even without a reward?
- What values am I teaching my students?
- How does this affect the relations among my students?

Summary of Main Points

❖ Excessive use of rewards and comparative praise can have a negative impact on the classroom climate and undermine cooperation.

❖ Positive expectations launch children in the direction of appropriate behavior.

❖ Honest, sincere, noncomparative praise given freely but not effusively can encourage cooperation.

❖ Rewards can sometimes be effective tools for correcting inappropriate behavior.

❖ Rewards should be used thoughtfully and sparingly.

4

Creating a Community
of Caring Listeners
and Talkers

*If we were supposed to talk more than we listen, we would
have two mouths and one ear.*

–Mark Twain

Many behavior problems erupt because students simply do not
know how to communicate with each other. Effective communication requires emotional intelligence, the ability to monitor one's
own and others' feelings and emotions, to discriminate among these
feelings, and to use this information to guide one's thinking and
actions (Salovey & Mayer, 1989-1990). Some children already pos-
sess emotional intelligence when they enter our classrooms. But
many do not. Every one of our students needs a solid amount of emotional intelligence if we are to maintain discipline in our classrooms
and if we are to succeed in guiding all of our students in becoming

responsible citizens. Because nobody suffers from having too much emotional intelligence—more just means happier, more successful living—when we provide classroom experiences that develop emotional intelligence, all students can benefit.

Is this just one more burden in our already overloaded schedule? Not at all. Developing our students' emotional intelligence and communication skills can actually lighten our load. Classroom discipline improves, life becomes more pleasant for everyone, and our students have the bonus of gaining in academic intelligence at the same time. There is solid research evidence that increased emotional intelligence improves academic achievement scores and school performance (Goleman, 1995).

We can make the task of helping our students develop more effective communication skills, and more emotional intelligence, a more manageable one if we break down the concept of emotional intelligence into several component skills: recognizing and labeling one's own feelings, recognizing and labeling the feelings of others, communicating one's feelings constructively, and listening to others. We can teach these skills separately.

As we discuss these skills, let's try to keep in mind how we can integrate them into the academic content we are currently teaching. It is amazing how beautifully they can be interwoven into literature, writing, social studies, art, and music. In addition, we can develop these skills in the course of daily living as issues and problems arise in the classroom. As John Dewey maintains, moral education is most potent when lessons are taught in the course of real events, not just in abstract lessons (Rockefeller, 1991).

Recognizing and Labeling Feelings

Three boys were playing ball when Ricardo came over and threw stones at them. Why? He felt left out. Alex whacked Troy when Troy deliberately banged into him in line. Why? He was angry. Regina spat at Gwen when Gwen teased her about her clothes. Why? She was embarrassed. Were these three children justified in their feelings? Absolutely! Being left out can be devastating. When someone deliberately bangs into you, it can be infuriating. And it certainly is embarrassing when someone makes fun of you. These are normal emotional reactions. As we know, we are all entitled to our feelings, whether they are positive or negative. That is part of what makes us human.

But were these children justified in choosing those actions to express their feelings? Absolutely not! Just because we feel bad about something does not entitle us to take it out on others. Another part of what makes us human and distinguishes us from animals is our ability to exercise self-control over our emotions and use words to express feelings.

Many children have no insight into what they or others are feeling. Nonempathic children are the source of many of our worst discipline nightmares. Because they don't understand their own feelings and how to express them constructively, their first response is often to lash out at others hurtfully to defend themselves. Because they lack insight into how other people feel, they can be cold and cruel in both their words and their actions. That's why it's so important to help our students develop empathy—for themselves and for others.

Students' Recognizing and Labeling Their Own Feelings

The first part of fostering empathy is to teach students how to use nonverbal clues to recognize their own feelings and how to express these feelings in words—for example, how they can realize when they are feeling angry, disappointed, anxious, sad, excited, or happy. Are they shaky? Tense? Tingly? Do they freeze up? What are their hands doing—banging, squeezing, trembling, relaxed? What is happening to their faces—their eyes, lips, nose, cheeks, eyebrows, forehead? What do they feel like inside? Having students act out their feelings during role play or in games such as charades, or having them look in mirrors or take and draw pictures of themselves, can help them to develop this personal insight so that they can acknowledge and express their own feelings.

Students' Recognizing and Labeling the Feelings of Others

The second part of fostering empathy is helping students tell when someone else is feeling angry, disappointed, anxious, sad, excited, or happy, for example. What do their faces, bodies, and hands look like? Looking at pictures and videos for signals of feelings can help children decipher the emotions of others. This skill can help prevent some of the fights that erupt because one child has misread another. "He looked like he was threatening me," or "She was smiling to make fun of me."

Suggested Activities

Curriculum Integration. Identifying and labeling feelings lends itself beautifully to curriculum integration, when the occasion arises naturally in the course of what we are already teaching.

Reading: Students can discuss how they think the characters felt. What words did the author use to describe their feelings? What clues did the author give as to how the characters might be feeling? How would you (the students) feel in a similar situation? Did you ever feel that way? What happened to make you feel like that?

Poetry: Poetry provides an excellent vehicle for students to gain emotional insight. Shel Silverstein's poems, for example, offer fertile ground for discussions of feelings (see Silverstein, 1974, 1981).

Science: Students can explore physical reactions to experiencing feelings, such as a faster heartbeat and increased perspiration.

Music: Students can listen to a musical selection to determine which emotions it is meant to convey and what are the distinguishing features of the music that convey these feelings. Students can also learn how to use music (loudness, tempo) to convey their emotions.

Art: The emotions portrayed in great works of art can be examined and students can learn how they can use art (colors, shapes, shading) to convey their emotions. A teacher named Lavonne McPherson introduced me to an art project where children gained tremendous insight into their own feelings as well as into those of others while developing their artistic and writing talents. Each student designed a papier-mâché feelings mask. After an introductory discussion, the students wrote about their feelings. Then, they planned on paper how they would symbolize their feelings on the mask. "This red bolt will show what I feel like when I get angry." "This blue circle will be for when I'm calm and enjoying myself." After making papier-mâché models of their faces, they painted their feelings symbols on the masks. Lavonne's students gained tremendous personal insight from having to think about their feelings, write about them, and then portray them symbolically.

Drama: Having students take on the role of another also teaches empathy. Students can act out parts in stories that they are reading.

Writing: Students can write a journal as if they were a character in history or in a novel discussing how they felt and why they felt that way. They can also illustrate the characters in stories or compose music to accompany a book.

Whatever the subject, by consciously attending to it, we can seamlessly weave identifying and labeling feelings into the curriculum. These are just a few suggestions. Each of us can come up with many other ways to accomplish this goal. Two excellent sources for ideas are *Reading, Thinking, and Caring (K-3)* and *Reading for Real (4-8)* published by Developmental Studies Center, Oakland, California, and *Number Power: A Cooperative Approach to Mathematics and Social Development* by L. Robertson.

Unstructured Times. Free time and recess also provide opportunities for introducing students to the language of feelings, without taking time away from instruction. Many games can be used during free time, transitional times, or recess to heighten awareness of feelings. Acting out feelings in charades gives students practice in recognizing nonverbal clues as well as experiencing the emotions they are acting out. Playing a dice game where each side of the die has the name or the picture of a different feeling, and the student discusses a time he or she felt the emotion displayed, helps students get things off their chests and develop personal insights into what bothers them. Guessing games where they practice facial expressions can be very beneficial to students who do not know how to give clear messages about how they are feeling. How can you let people know how you are feeling? Do you squint your eyes? Clench your fists? Shake? Wrinkle your brow? Many teachers find that Polaroid cameras are helpful for these activities. Watching videotapes or movies on a rainy day with the sound off, or with people speaking a foreign language, can teach students to attend to nonverbal clues of emotions. During transition times that might otherwise be wasted, brainstorming how many different words students can find for the same or similar emotions (such as *happy, glad, joyous, thrilled*) can expand their emotional insight and vocabulary simultaneously.

Classroom Routines. The skill of learning how to identify and label feelings can also become part of the daily classroom routine. In the PATHS (Promoting Alternative Thinking Strategies) curriculum based in Seattle, Washington, students attach feeling faces to strips that say "I feel . . ." to express their feelings during the school day. Not only do students learn to express their own emotions, but they develop empathy for others this way (Greenberg & Kusche, 1993). If a student posts that he or she is sad or lonely, others may reach out to him or her. In the Self-Science Program at the Nueva Learning Center, students call out how they feel on a scale of 1 to 10 (Stone & Dillehunt, 1978). In other schools, teachers find it helpful to have students write about how they are feeling that day during morning seatwork. This provides a teacher with a barometer of the child's mood for the day and the child has the opportunity to develop personal awareness as well as writing skills. Another teacher has a transition activity in which she periodically passes around an object—such as a smooth stone—and has the students take their feelings temperature with it, discussing how they are feeling at the time.

Talking about feelings is often far more difficult for boys than for girls. Girls seem to be more adept at reading nonverbal and verbal signals and at expressing and communicating feelings (Gilligan, 1993). Boys tend to be more active than girls and are also more likely to respond physically when distressed. That's one reason why physical aggression is a more common discipline problem among male students than among female students. Therefore, our efforts in helping our male students develop a vocabulary of emotion may have to be more concentrated.

By helping students become aware of their own feelings, and then of the feelings of others, we are planting the seed of empathy, a critical ingredient for the ethic of care (Gilligan, 1993) and, therefore, for peaceful, harmonious living. When children are unaware of their own feelings, then "feelings" are a foreign concept to them. They hit others and laugh, smirk when one of their classmates is crying, and continue playing as if nothing happened when someone gets hurt on the playground. Children who lack empathy can hurt others without seeming to care because *hurt, frightened,* and *sad* are meaningless terms to them. Having no feelings for themselves or others, these children suffer no remorse. The roots of morality are in empathy (Hoffman, 1984).

Communicating Feelings Nonhurtfully

As students develop a vocabulary of feelings, our next step is to help them express these feelings constructively. One way to do this is by using the "I Message."

I Messages

There are two kinds of I Messages; one is just to disclose one's feelings or opinion and the other is to try to bring about change in another's behavior.

Self-Disclosure. The goal of the first kind of I Message is self-disclosure. The speaker just wants to let someone know how he or she is feeling or what he or she is thinking. "When we have no homework on Friday, I am so happy because I have a lot of things I want to do on the weekend." "When you lent me your pencil, I was so relieved." "I am sorry that your dog died." "I appreciate how you feel. I'm afraid of the dark also." "I'm excited that we're going on the field trip." "I'm annoyed that I can't have another piece." "I disagree with that interpretation." "I enjoyed the walk." Encouraging our students to express a variety of feelings and opinions can help develop their emotional intelligence and a sense of connectedness to others. Class meetings, discussed on pages 23-25, provide an excellent opportunity for students to practice this skill, as do writing workshops where students provide feedback to each other about their writing (see Resource A).

To Change Behavior. The goal of the second kind of I Message is to make a change in someone's behavior because it interferes with our needs. It is designed to effect positive change, not just to express one's feelings. This kind of I Message provides an alternative to lashing out at others verbally or physically when they are doing something that is interfering with our needs and when we want them to change. This kind of I Message fits into a fairly simple three-part formula that we can model for our students: (a) describing the behavior, (b) letting the person know how the behavior made you feel, and (c) letting the person know the consequences of the behavior for you. In Chapter 5, we discuss in detail how we teachers can use I Messages to deal with certain discipline problems and, in so doing, be a model for this approach. In addition to our modeling the process, we can directly teach students the three components of the I Message and, even if students don't master all three parts of the I Message formula, we may inspire them to think about the reasons for their feelings. At the very least, they will develop a general idea of how to express their emotions constructively.

"When . . ." Teaching students to use the word *when* can help them describe the behavior that they dislike and want to change. Using the word *when* helps students narrow the problem to a specific situation rather than implying that it's always a problem. For example, "When I am interrupted . . ." We are more likely to consider changing our behavior if we consider it to be manageable because it is limited to a specific situation.

This should be done without accusing or blaming so that the listener is not put on the defensive. That is why it's important to help students avoid the accusatory "you" when constructing this part of an I Message. Instead, we can help them describe the situation that is upsetting them in neutral terms without blaming another child, thereby avoiding confrontation. For example, "When I can't play in the block area . . ." rather than "When you hog the block area," or "When my crayons are broken . . ." rather than "When you are so sloppy you break my crayons," or "When I'm left out . . ." rather than "You're so mean!"

"I Feel . . ." After describing the behavior they want changed, our students should let the listener know how they feel. Help them try to avoid general words such as *angry* and *mad* and get to the feelings that lie below the anger (see Chapter 5 for further discussion). Help them try to get to the emotion that lies at the heart of what they're feeling and to be honest about it. "I feel left out"; "It makes me feel sad"; "I get confused"; "I worry"; "I was disappointed"; or "I get scared." Better yet, "When I'm interrupted, I get confused . . ."

"Because . . ." Help students explain how the situation tangibly and concretely affects them. This sells their message. *Because* helps students justify their feelings to their peers: They have a good reason for feeling sad, hurt, or left out. For example, "When I'm interrupted, I get confused because I forget what I am saying." "When my crayons are broken, I feel frustrated because I can't make thin lines when I need to." "When I'm not allowed to have my turn in the block area, I am disappointed because it's my favorite thing to do." "When I'm not allowed to join the game, I feel very left out and sad because then I have no one to play with."

I Messages help our students express their feelings in a way that often enables them to meet their own objective. Listeners are much more responsive and are more likely to react in a helpful manner if they are approached with an I Message rather than with accusatory language or physical aggression. One's tone of voice in giving an I Message greatly influences its effectiveness. Listening to foreign language tapes and role-playing provide excellent practice for helping students develop proper tone and have the tone reflect their true feelings. If they're disappointed, their voice should show it. Students can practice making their voices firm and direct without being intimidating and harsh when they are upset.

Listening to Others

The ability to listen to another, to understand what another is saying and where he or she is coming from, is another essential skill for developing relationships and connectedness. This skill compliments the ability to identify and label feelings. Poor listening is the source of a good number of discipline problems. Because they don't hear each other out, children often jump to incorrect conclusions and attack one another.

Listening Skills for Students

Here, too, there are skills that we can directly teach our students so that they can become good listeners:

1. How to listen with their eyes as well as their ears to detect nonverbal clues, such as facial expression and body language.

Often bodies more accurately express what we are feeling than do words.

2. How to show interest. How to stay focused on the person speaking so that he or she will know we are paying attention.

3. How to hear someone out. Giving the speaker enough time to express his or her ideas before jumping in with our side of the story or jumping to conclusions can be a challenge.

Activities for Practicing Listening Skills

The following are some ways that we can help students practice these skills and promote good listening. I am sure you can come up with many more creative ideas as well.

- Listening games, such as Telephone, can be used during transitional times. One person whispers something into another's ear, that person whispers the message to the next person, and so on. After the message has traveled from ear to ear, the last person says the message aloud. Usually, what the last person heard bears little resemblance to the original message. This is a great opportunity to discuss the listening process with students and show how messages can get distorted by poor listening skills.

- Have a sharing time when students listen to each other's writing and provide feedback.

- Assign oral class reports.

- Have another kind of sharing time, such as "show-and-tell," when students discuss events in their lives. Having students say to each other, "Tell me more about your favorite hobby," or "Tell me what you liked about it" gives them the opportunity to practice giving feedback.

- Group projects presented to the class provide opportunities for students to practice their listening skills.

- Listening to books and music in foreign languages can help develop skills in listening for tone as well as for words.

- Using examples from newscasters who are interviewing people, we can teach students how to be good listeners—how to maintain eye contact, how to hold their bodies in a receptive fashion, and how to detect nonverbal clues of the speaker.

- Role-playing is also particularly effective for practicing listening skills.
- Writing workshops can help develop students' writing skills and can also help develop their listening and empathic skills. After students have written in their writing folders, they gather together and those who choose to do so share their writing. After listening to what their classmates have written, students can learn how to provide positive feedback. "I like your choice of descriptive words for that sentence. I could really picture what she looked like." "The story really grabbed my attention." In addition, the interest they show by asking questions about the writing can also be reinforcing. "Why did you choose to have the story take place there?" "What do you plan to write next?" Of course, students will need our guidance at first on how to provide the feedback and what kinds of questions to ask, but it doesn't take long for them to catch on (see Resource A for more information on writing workshops).

After we awaken our student's feelings and empathy for others, we can help them learn how to express their own feelings and how to listen to others express their feelings in a truly caring fashion. Communication is the key for sustaining a web of caring relationships (Gilligan, 1993), which results in a more peaceful classroom.

Communication, Collaboration, and Cooperation

Now let's look at how we can provide structured classroom opportunities for our students to practice effective communication skills. Discussions on rules (Chapter 2), class meetings where students make decisions (Chapter 8), writing workshops (see above), participation in classroom chores (Chapter 1), and problem solving (Chapter 8) encourage communication, cooperation, and collaboration among students. In addition, cooperative learning activities and small group projects can help students learn how to get along with each other and to work together toward a common goal. But we can do this only if we guide students by assigning tasks to each member of the group and practicing with them over and over again communication etiquette, including how to listen and how to provide constructive feedback. The Child Development Project provides an excellent model for designing cooperative learning situations for students that are truly cooperative rather than competitive. See Resource B for further information on this program and others.

Community service projects also teach responsibility and develop the ethic of care. Whether students adopt a younger class to read to once a week, participate in a schoolwide beautification program, or undertake a community service project, they are learning the joys of reaching out to help others, and their self-worth receives a tremendous boost. They think "I'm needed," "I'm wanted." Children learn to pull together, work cooperatively toward a common goal, and develop caring and empathy in the process. For a wealth of ideas for social service and community projects, see Barbara Lewis's books *The Kid's Guide to Social Action* (Lewis, 1991) and *The Kid's Guide to Service Projects: Over 500 Service Ideas for Young People Who Want to Make a Difference* (Lewis, 1995).

Caring Teacher Listening:
A Preventive Discipline Tool

Just as listening is a tool for achieving connectedness among students, so too is it a tool for us to achieve connectedness with our students. Listening to our students has important benefits. First, if we listen, our students will likely observe and imitate our behavior. Second, by listening, we will know better what our students are thinking and feeling. Third, many discipline problems can be avoided if we don't jump to conclusions but rather take the time to listen and hear the whole story. Fourth, we establish a good rapport with our students by making them feel that what they have to say is important and that they matter. Sometimes just listening defuses and solves problems. Listening is one sign of our caring.

How to Listen

Show Our Interest. Interest is conveyed by body language. Sometimes we say we are listening but our bodies say otherwise. Consider the following example: Devon had ripped another child's paper and wanted to tell the teacher his side of the story. "Well, go ahead," she responded and stood there, arms folded across her chest, foot tapping, and rolling her eyes. She told him, "go ahead" but was she really communicating interest? Her unspoken message was, "Get it over with already."

If a child has to follow us as we move around the room, if we are writing while we are listening, if we keep looking at the clock, or if we have a supremely bored expression on our face, what will our students conclude? Probably that we really are not very interested in their ideas. What is the end result? Frustration and resentment. They might think, "Why should I even bother telling her?" What will they learn from our behavior? "What's the use?" "She's not listening to me. She doesn't care."

Our actions often speak louder than our words. We can be sure that our students know we are listening and focusing on them when we look at them, nod our heads in understanding, and insert an occasional comment that reflects that we hear what they are saying, "I see you found . . ." or "Okay, so you're saying . . ."

Hear Them Out. Effective listening means taking the time to hear a student out without jumping to premature conclusions and trying to finish his or her sentences. Because we are so pressed for time, it is sometimes hard to stop and hear the whole long story. But can't we get ourselves into trouble if we jump to conclusions? Let's see what happened to this teacher:

Mr. Hale: Travis, stop running in the hall.

Travis: But, Mr. Hale, I can't . . .

Mr. Hale: Don't but me. Stop that running right now!

Travis: But . . .

Mr. Hale: Young man, do you want to go to the principal's office?

Unfortunately, Travis never got the chance to tell Mr. Hale that someone was hurt on the playground and he was running to get ice from the cafeteria. Imagine Travis's frustration! Imagine his resentment to Mr. Hale! Imagine Mr. Hale's embarrassment and guilt when he found out what had actually happened!

All of us can understand why Mr. Hale might have reacted the way he did. With 25 to 30 students pulling us in different directions, it's hard to concentrate on what one child is saying. But hearing a child out often only takes a minute or two and it may save an hour or two down the road. When children feel that they are not listened to, they may continuously nag or be distracted from their studies because their concern is still on their mind. Let's look at how much easier it would have been had Mr. Hale taken the time to hear Travis out.

Mr. Hale: Travis, stop running in the hall

Travis: But Mr. Hale, I can't . . .

Mr. Hale: Why, is something wrong?

Travis: Yes, Jameel fell and his lip was swelling up badly and my teacher told me to get ice as fast as I could.

Or better yet, he could have tried to tune into Travis's body language and pick up on his tension.

Mr. Hale: Travis, is there something wrong?

Travis: Yes, Jameel fell and his lip was swelling up badly and my teacher told me to get ice as fast as I could.

As in this case, sometimes the fastest route is just to hear a child out. In other situations, when we absolutely cannot stop what we are doing, we may be able to suggest to the child an alternative time when we can listen to all he or she has to say.

Hearing a student out also means trying not to interject our own solutions or advice. For example, a child comes running to her teacher complaining that her best friend won't play with her. Our first tendency might be to respond in one of these ways: "So play with someone else"; "Maybe she'll play with you tomorrow"; "Help me erase the board"; or "We've got to go in now anyway." Quick answers like these may seem like the easiest and fastest way to deal with the problem, especially if we are in a hurry or consider the problem to be trivial, but usually the problem keeps festering because the root issue remains unresolved. How do you feel when you tell someone about a problem you're having and right away they jump into giving you unsolicited advice or change the subject? Instead, when hearing a child out, we can help that child by reflecting back to him or her: "Gee, that must have been disappointing," or "I'm sorry to hear that.

You must have been upset about that." Empathizing with the child, but leaving the solution in his or her hands, helps prevent us from getting sucked into the situation and giving advice that might not work and then being blamed for it.

Sometimes, hearing a student out can totally change how we see things. Consider this example: Students are not allowed to have snacks in Ms. Ford's class. One afternoon, she discovered Alonzo scarfing down a bag of potato chips. "Put them away or I'll throw them out," decreed Ms. Ford. "But . . . ," he pleaded. "No buts, just put them away." When Alonzo kept eating, his teacher threw the chips in the basket. Alonzo became violent and had to be carried out of the classroom, crying and flailing his arms.

The whole nasty scene could have been avoided had Ms. Ford just listened to what came after Alonzo's "But." Alonzo was taking medication each morning at school for behavior problems. Because his medication took away his appetite, he had not eaten breakfast or lunch. By 2:00, he was starving. He ate whatever he could find—the chips. If we hadn't eaten all day and someone threw our food in the trash, wouldn't we be furious?

Ms. Ford could have let Alonzo go to the cafeteria or somewhere else out of the sight of the other children and allowed him to eat some healthy food. One might ask, But what if the teacher had a rule about no eating? Yes, students should learn to obey classroom rules, but sometimes we just have to be flexible about when it is appropriate to break a rule. It would be wise for Ms. Ford to contact Alonzo's parents and discuss the effects of the medication. Perhaps his parents could speak to their physician and get the medication adjusted.

Separate Our Feelings From Their Feelings. It is critical that when our students are upset and express their distress to us, we do not blur the line between our feelings and their feelings and start to get upset or become defensive ourselves. Isn't it better for both us and our students if we try not to overreact and control our own emotions?

Sean hadn't completed his homework and was told that he had to complete it during recess. He barged up to his teacher, slapped his hands across his chest, and in an angry voice said, "It's not fair. Alice didn't do her homework and she can go out to recess. You make me stay in all the time because you don't like me." The teacher shot back in an angry tone, "Don't tell me how to treat other students. It's your own fault. If you just did your work, you wouldn't have so many

problems." Sean stomped off, fuming even more, and the teacher to
him he'd miss the next day's recess as well for being so angry.

The teacher could have defused the whole situation by remaining
calm, focusing on Sean's feelings, and keeping him- or herself out of
it. The teacher didn't have to defend his or her actions with Sean. All
that was needed was to acknowledge his feelings. "It may not seem
fair to you, but your situations are different" or "I'm sorry you're
disappointed. How could you help yourself remember to complete
your homework?" This approach would have taken the wind out of
his sails without giving in to him and would have helped him to face
reality.

When our students get annoyed at us, it's easy for us to react
defensively: "Don't tell me how to run my class, young lady"; "You
have no right to complain. You got what you deserved"; or "Don't
blame me; it's not my fault you didn't do your work." But these
responses can be counterproductive. The student stays angry, we stay
angry, resentment continues, and communication is compromised.

Look for Nonverbal Clues. How do you think the child feels who
says, "My teacher was absent today"? There's absolutely no way to tell
unless we consider the child's facial expression, body language, and tone
of voice. The very same words may signify disappointment or glee, or
they may be nothing more than a statement of fact. Try to notice a
student's body language: Is he stiff and tense? Does she seem threatened? What does his face look like? What's her tone of voice? What is
the message he is trying to convey with his body as well as with his
words?

Put Their Feelings Into Words. Picking up and reflecting back the
child's feelings in words helps him or her develop a vocabulary of
feelings: "That must have made you feel uncomfortable." "It sounds as
though you're upset." "It sounds like you're disappointed." If we've
labeled the feeling incorrectly, they'll let us know. For example, "No,
I'm scared."

I have found that putting students' feelings into words and
reflecting back to them can work miracles with tattlers. Tattlers can
drive us crazy. Erin had a constant litany of complaints: "Raoul
pushed me." "Tammy took my pencil." "Davis is drawing on Juanita's
paper." No matter how many times her teacher told her "Stop tattling,
I don't want to hear it," "Why don't you mind your own business,"

or "Just sit down," for whatever reason, she kept coming up with more tales. Erin's teacher attended a workshop where I addressed this issue and decided to try this new approach of reflecting back Erin's feelings. "That bothers you?" or "I can see that upsets you" became her responses to Erin's tales, and within a couple of weeks, the tattling had stopped. Why? Because Erin saw that it didn't bother her teacher. She was hoping that the tattling would bother her teacher so that her teacher would find fault with the other children. Maybe she didn't like the other child. Perhaps the child was the teacher's pet. Matter-of-factly reflecting back Erin's feelings completely stopped the tattling.

A 7-year-old child came running up to her teacher crying that another child told her she couldn't read. Her initial thought was to say either, "You know that's not true—you can read" or "Where is she [the other girl]? Let me speak to her." But the teacher decided to try a new approach: "I'm sure that hurt your feelings when she said that to you." "It hurt my feelings. I know I can read and I felt stupid when everyone around us heard her." The girl then asked if she could read to the teacher, and the discussion ended on a positive note.

By listening to their message and putting their feelings into words, we can help our students understand their own emotions, cope with them, find their own solutions, and thus help them become more emotionally intelligent.

Putting our students' feelings into words as we listen to them does not mean that we have to agree with the feelings. We just have to agree that they have a right to their feelings, whatever they are. Sometimes their feelings seem totally ridiculous to us: fury over not being first in line, rage because they don't have the right color crayon, or fear of the fire alarm. Sometimes, we may feel uncomfortable with their feelings. However, it's not up to us to be judgmental. It's our job to be a sounding board, not a judge and jury. With the sounding board of a good listener, students can generally come to their own conclusions. When bad feelings come out, there's more room inside for good feelings to surface.

Nicholas came storming into the classroom one morning, plopped himself down at his desk, and pouted. His teacher came up to him, knelt down to his eye level, and said,

Teacher: Seems like you've had a rough morning.
Nicholas: I sure have.

Teacher: Something must have gone wrong.

Nicholas: Everything went wrong. My parents were screaming at each other, my older brother was teasing me, and I couldn't find my jeans.

Teacher: That must have been a difficult time for you.

Nicholas: It sure was.

Nicholas left his teacher, hung up his coat, and got busy with work. All Nicholas needed was a listening ear to get him back on a positive track.

Don't Argue With Their Feelings. If something were bothering us and we felt down about it and a friend said, "Cheer up. There's no need to be upset," or "What's the big deal? Come on, you don't really have to feel that way," how would it make us feel? Wouldn't we consider it an insult? In addition to our first reason for feeling badly, we would now have another reason—that we are told our feelings don't matter to our friend or that our feelings are wrong.

We may not necessarily agree with how children feel, or we may think they're ridiculous for feeling that way, but it's important to accept their right to feel as they do. Arguing with feelings is a no-win proposition and can even spoil our relationship with them.

Tips for Effective Listening

The following are some tips for listening so that we can work with the grain of the wood instead of against it:

1. Show our interest. Pay attention when students speak. Stay focused on them without trying to do 10 other things at the same time. Give them feedback to show we get the message.
2. Hear them out. Give them enough time to speak and wait until they are through before we say anything. Don't jump to conclusions.
3. Separate our personal feelings from theirs. Don't overreact. Don't take their outbursts personally. Try to stay focused on the issue and not on our personal reactions.
4. Look for nonverbal clues in trying to figure out the message being conveyed. Be aware of body language that might clue us into the true meaning behind the words.

5. Try to put their message and feelings into words. Try to rephrase what we think they are feeling, but try to avoid just echoing their words. If we don't pinpoint the correct feeling, they'll let us know. Then we can accept their correction and perhaps try again to figure out what they are feeling.

6. Be a good model and express our own feelings in our daily interactions.

Summary of Main Points

❖ Poor communication is the source of many discipline problems.

❖ Effective communication requires emotional intelligence.

❖ Recognizing and labeling feelings, communicating feelings non-hurtfully, and listening to others are skills we can teach our students to develop their emotional intelligence.

❖ Rule setting, classroom meetings, writing workshops, problem solving, cooperative learning, and group projects help the class become a caring community.

❖ Listening is an important preventive discipline tool for caring teachers.

5

Harnessing and Channeling Anger Into Constructive Outlets

Anyone can become angry. That's easy. But to be angry at the right person to the right degree at the right time for the right purpose and in the right way, that is not easy.

—Aristotle

Anger can create an unpleasant, tense undercurrent in the classroom. Angry students physically lash out at others, utter cruel and harsh words, and deliberately provoke us and their classmates. Teaching students how to manage and harness their anger is a crucial discipline tool.

Defusing Student Anger on the Spot

Sometimes we need to take immediate action to defuse a student's anger before that student does something hurtful to him- or herself or to others. But trying to squelch anger by threatening a punishment if the student doesn't calm down or by just telling the student not to be angry will very likely exacerbate the problem. Instead, I have found the following approach to be incredibly successful.

Acknowledge the Anger

Sometimes just acknowledging a student's feelings and his or her right to have these feelings is enough to resolve the problem. Don't we all need to vent at times? Just getting our feelings out of our system can be so therapeutic. All we want is someone to acknowledge our right to feel the way we feel. Let's look what happens in these two scenarios:

Kara crumples up her paper, throws it in the trash, and stomps back to her seat.

> **Ms. Lucas:** What's that all about?
> **Kara:** Nothing.
> **Ms. Lucas:** Well, if it's nothing young lady, take that paper out of the basket and continue writing on it.

Kara pouts during the rest of the lesson and gets no work done.

> **Ms. Lucas:** Well it's your choice, Kara. If you don't do the work, you'll have to miss recess today and make up your work.

Now, let's look at the same scene with the teacher listening and acknowledging Kara's anger:

Kara crumples up her paper, throws it in the trash, and stomps back to her seat. Ms. Lucas goes over to Kara's desk.

> **Ms. Lucas:** Kara, that upset you. Apparently the paper displeased you.

Kara: Yes it did. My pencil tip broke and it made my paper look all messy.

Ms. Lucas: It sounds like you must have been embarrassed by how it looked.

Kara: Yes, I was. But I'll start another one now.

It didn't take any more time for the teacher to acknowledge how Kara was feeling, but it sure saved them both a lot of aggravation. The teacher-student rapport was improved and both teacher and student saved face.

Helpful Tips for Acknowledging Anger

- Stay calm. Don't take their anger personally. Being frightened or wounded by a student's anger gives the student too much power.
- Allow them to express their feelings rather than trying to change them: "So you're feeling hurt . . ." rather than "Come on, you don't really feel that way."
- Accept their feelings without arguing about their reasoning: "So you feel that . . ." rather than "You don't have a right to feel that way because . . ." or "You shouldn't feel hurt. . . ."

Ask Guiding Questions

Although sometimes just allowing a student to vent and express his or her feelings is enough to resolve the situation, at other times we can use our listening skills to help guide our students to figuring out solutions to the problem that infuriated them in the first place. Our listening can become more active. After reflecting back their feelings to them and letting them know that we hear them, we can ask guiding questions. For example, "What seems to be the problem?" "What do you think you can do about it?" "Which solution do you think would work best?" This problem-solving approach is discussed in greater detail in Chapter 8.

Consider a situation where the students have just come in from recess:

Mr. Powell: Please sit down and begin writing in your folder.

Several students are still wandering around the room.

> **Mr. Powell:** If you are not seated by the time I count to 10, you'll have to sit out the last 5 minutes of the next recess so you'll be settled down by the time you return to class.

Latanya is still standing by her desk at the count of 10.

> **Mr. Powell:** Latanya, you owe me 5 minutes at the next recess.
> **Latanya:** But that's not fair!

Latanya slouches in her desk, pouting, fuming.

> **Mr. Powell:** I gave you fair warning. You have no right to be angry. Just settle down and get to work.

Latanya mumbles several foul words under her breath and doesn't write one single word in her writing folder. The next round of the Latanya-Mr. Powell bout was about to begin.

Trying to stifle Latanya's anger created an even greater discipline problem. Let's look at how this situation could have been defused by giving Latanya a voice:

> **Mr. Powell:** Latanya, next recess, you need to make up the time you wasted.
> **Latanya:** But that's not fair!

Latanya slouches in her desk, pouting, fuming. Mr. Powell goes over to Latanya's desk and crouches down.

> **Mr. Powell:** I can see that you're upset.
> **Latanya:** I didn't do anything wrong. I always stand when I get out my writing folder.
> **Mr. Powell:** Did you not have enough time to get out the folder?
> **Latanya:** No, it takes me a while.
> **Mr. Powell:** I wonder why you feel it takes you longer than anyone else?

Latanya: I guess because I was talking to Kay while I did it.

Mr. Powell: How do you think you could help yourself to do it faster next time?

Latanya: I'll tell Kay I can't talk until I get my folder out.

Did Mr. Powell agree with Latanya? Of course not. Many times, students' anger may seem unjustified or even silly to us. It would be absurd to agree with them. Sometimes, all we have to do is give them a sounding board so that they can get the anger out of their system and then guide them to solving their problem.

In the case of a raging, out-of-control child, acknowledging anger and asking guiding questions may be impossible. In that case, we can use our body language to help calm the situation. The key is not to assume a threatening demeanor. Here are a few suggestions:

- Keep our hands visible so that the child doesn't fear what's behind our backs.
- Assume a nonthreatening posture by keeping our hands unfolded with our palms visible.
- Respect the child's personal space by keeping a reasonable distance, up to 3 feet, to minimize his or her fear of us.
- Avoid a staring match so that no one assumes a combative stance.
- Try not to appear overpowering. Stoop or sit down if necessary to be at the child's level.
- Unless we must physically restrain a child to prevent that child from hurting him- or herself, or from hurting someone else, then avoiding physical contact works best in these situations. If we have to touch the child, the shoulder and the wrist would be the most effective places (Polowy, 1992).

Helping Students Harness Anger

We have just discussed how to deal with angry outbursts on the spot. Now let's explore how we can minimize them. All human beings get angry at times. Anger, like happiness and sadness, is a normal human emotion. People cannot control their feelings of anger any more than they can control their feelings of happiness, joy, sadness, or frustration. Feelings just are. Anger is neither a good nor a bad thing. What is "good" or "bad" is the way we handle the anger we feel (Prothrow-Stith & Weissman, 1991). Everyone, including our students, is entitled to angry feelings just as they are entitled to other feelings. But no one, including our students, is entitled to angry actions, such as lashing out at others verbally or physically. Let's explore how we can help students learn in three steps how to express and channel their anger constructively and nonhurtfully by teaching them anger-harnessing skills.

Psychologist Haim Ginott once said that just as the time to teach someone how to swim is not when that person is drowning, the time to teach someone how to harness his or her anger is not when that person is raging mad. It's most helpful to pick a quiet time to introduce some of these steps and directly teach the steps. We can also weave these skills into daily living and integrate them into our curriculum as well.

Step One: Awareness

Self-Awareness. Someone bumps into Andy, he gets infuriated, and his hand lashes out. Lisa shoots out a whole litany of cuss words when she feels she has been wronged. Rella throws things when she gets angry. In order for these children to change what they are doing and to learn how to express their anger in an alternative fashion, they need to become aware of when they feel rage coming on so that they can catch themselves before they "lose it."

Our bodies have extraordinary ways of letting us know when we are angry and are about to lose control. Tensed muscles, grinding teeth, clenched fists, flushing in the face, goose bumps, shakiness, shivering, twitching, sweating, changing body temperature (hot/cold), laughing, crying, and stony silence are among the ways that our bodies signal our anger. When students learn to identify their own personal anger signals, they can begin to detect that angry feeling before it overtakes them. They can stop and think before they act.

Many academic subjects can serve as excellent vehicles for heightening the awareness of the negative effects of angry feelings on our bodies and our actions.

Literature: Discussions could include questions such as these: "How do you think the character looked when he was so angry?" "What's the description of his face?" "Describe what you think his body felt like." "Think about a time when you felt that way." "Think about what your body felt like." "How do you think you look when you're angry?" "How can you tell when you're about to get angry?" Also, books such as *Alexander and the Terrible, Horrible, No Good Very Bad Day*, by Judith Viorst, and Judy Blume's books are excellent takeoff points for a discussion on anger and other feelings.

Writing: Writing about their own personal experiences of anger, such as what makes them angry, their maddest moment, or their pet peeve, can help students improve their writing and deal with people more appropriately. Of course, they may choose not to share this writing with the class.

Social studies: Exploring expressions of anger among different peoples can be instructive for students. Some cultures discourage outward expressions of anger, whereas others encourage letting it all hang out. World events can be discussed in terms of anger, such as how anger often leads to war.

Transition times: Activities such as charades, taking photographs, and making faces in mirrors can heighten children's awareness of their bodily responses and are great transition time fillers.

These curricular activities can help students identify their own anger signals and allow them to detect when they are about to fly off the handle and then stop themselves from doing something that they will later regret.

Awareness of Others. In addition to not being able to catch themselves before they lash out in anger, many of our most troublesome discipline problems arise because children misread each other: "You looked like you were going to hit me." "I could see that you were angry at me." "Don't you dis me." Many times, students perceive slights when none are intended. They imagine peers to be more hostile than they are and interpret neutral situations as being threatening (Lochman, Dunn, & Klimes-Dougan, 1993). That is why learning how to "read" other people is important. The same kinds of activities that work for self-awareness (see above) will also work for awareness of others. Students can learn how to look, stop, assess the situation, and think before they react.

Step Two: Collecting Themselves

This step is designed to help students de-escalate. Angry feelings and actions can escalate and intensify quite rapidly. Anger feeds on itself and unchecked anger snowballs. That's why it is so important to help our students become calm. But what happens when someone tells you to "calm down" when you're angry? Usually, it just makes you even more angry. "Why should I calm down? I have a right to be angry." "Don't tell me what to do." Rather than tell our students to calm down, we can guide them to specific strategies that they can use to collect themselves:

Physical exercise: Exercise can help eliminate tension. Once the exercise stops, the body rebounds to a low arousal level. Jumping jacks, jumping rope, running around the track, and working out are all great releases. Of course, this kind of exercise isn't feasible in the middle of a lesson, but there are other times when it may be possible.

Separation: Sometimes it helps just to get away from the anger-provoking situation for a few minutes. Many teachers have found it helpful to have a time-out corner where children can go to collect themselves. This kind of time-out is designed to give students an opportunity to collect their thoughts, take a break from a heated situation, and calm themselves down. We can let our students know that it is designed as an aid in anger management and not as a punishment for anger. Punishing students for feelings, including anger, will only make students more angry, hostile, and resentful.

Distraction: Listening to music, reading, drawing, scribbling, or writing can prevent anger from snowballing. Attention is diverted away from the anger and the activities themselves are calming. These activities can take place in the time-out corner.

Soothing activities: Deep breathing and counting backward from 10 are convenient ways for children to collect themselves in the classroom. All of our students, not just the very angry ones, could benefit from learning these techniques. The gentle back and forth of a rocking chair can extinguish the flames of anger.

Constructive activities: Building or making something can be helpful to some children. Manipulatives that keep their hands busy can be an excellent distracter. Twisting and turning something concrete like clay can release negative energy. Clay and some building materials could be placed in the time-out corner.

A note of caution: It's best to avoid suggesting punching pillows, spitting out angry thoughts, or screaming as techniques for the calming-down stage. Some maintain that these approaches help children "get it out of their system." But current brain research advises against techniques that pump up the emotional brain's arousal because they leave the person even more angry (Tice & Baumeister, 1993). Our goal is to get the student calm enough to be able to verbalize his or her anger in a rational way.

Step Three: Talking and Labeling Their Feelings

This step teaches students how to constructively express anger. Once the student has cooled down, he or she should have the clarity of mind to be able to put his or her feelings into words and try to resolve the situation: "I was afraid that I might do it wrong." "I was embarrassed when they made fun of me." "I felt I deserved the sticker, not him." Through reflective listening, we can draw out their feelings and guide them to labeling the primary feeling that lies below the surface of anger, perhaps jealousy, nervousness, loneliness, discouragement, disappointment, embarrassment, fear, worry, humiliation, or sadness.

Anger is often a blanket that covers up many other feelings. What lies below the fury of the child who rips up his or her paper because he or she made a mistake? Fear of failure. What is the child feeling who lashes out after being teased? Embarrassment. Helplessness.

Why is the student steaming because the field trip is canceled? Disappointment. Through reflective listening, we can guide the angry child to these insights: For example, "It sounds like you were afraid that if you made mistakes you wouldn't pass," or "You sure seemed disappointed when we couldn't go on the field trip."

Summary: Harnessing Anger

We can expect that anger will surface in our classrooms. We can also expect this anger to be a loose cannon unless we help students learn how to deal with it constructively:

- Recognize the signs of anger in themselves and in others.
- Develop techniques for collecting themselves and de-escalating their feelings.
- Verbalize in a nonhurtful manner the primary feelings that lie below their anger.

In so doing, we can prevent many potential discipline problems from occurring.

Preventing Student Anger

Feelings of powerlessness lie at the heart of much student anger. By understanding that, we can try to give our students feelings of empowerment within the classroom. In so doing, we can prevent some anger from ever erupting in the first place.

Understanding What Makes Students Angry

Some children are angry the moment they enter our classrooms. We can practically see the steam rising. Their anger may have nothing whatsoever to do with us or their classmates but, rather, stems from their helplessness and powerlessness in their lives beyond the classroom. Anger shields them against feeling powerless in a situation where they feel threatened. A sense of endangerment, whether it be an actual physical threat or a symbolic threat to one's self-esteem, is a universal trigger for anger (Zillman, 1993).

Child Abuse. Many abused children fester with rage. Isn't anger a normal and, in fact, a healthy response to being deliberately hurt by someone else? But how can abused children possibly express their anger at those who mistreat them? They would risk even further mistreatment. So they submerge their anger into cauldrons boiling deep within them, venting steam on "safe" targets: us and other students.

Societal Rage. Class and race discrimination have hindered many groups from achieving success. Some children have had drilled into them the belief that the deck is stacked against them. Many seem perpetually irritable. They are sure that "the system," including teachers, has it in for them and that they have no hope (Prothrow-Stith & Weissman, 1991). They, too, feel powerless and inadequate.

Trauma. Many children have suffered from major traumatic losses, for example, the death of a parent or sibling, witnessing violence, or being in an accident. Anger is a common initial response to traumatic loss because the victim is totally helpless to prevent the tragedy.

Normal Living. Even children who do not have all this baggage often react with anger when they feel helpless—when they fear failure, when they are humiliated by put-downs or ridicule, when they think they have been treated unjustly by another, when they suspect dishonesty, or when they are not allowed to express their feelings. Some are supersensitive and overreact to any feedback or criticism. Most people, adults and children alike, respond with anger when they feel they have been robbed of their power.

Empowering Students

Because powerlessness or helplessness lies at the root of much of our students' anger, let's explore how we can structure our classroom to empower them. By designing positive sources of power for students and by trying to avoid situations where students feel powerless, we can both dramatically reduce the likelihood of triggering angry responses in students who are encumbered by extra baggage and avoid many of the daily hassles and annoyances that occur with all of our students. Let's explore some positive sources of power:

Choice. By giving students choices among acceptable options, we can maintain our control yet give them a sense of power and control as well. They have a choice, but only from the options we choose. We define the parameters. What are some empowering choices students can make while still meeting our objectives?

- The order in which they do their morning seatwork or other work or which book to read from a list of suggested books
- What to write about given some guidelines or general parameters or whom to sit with at lunch
- Which of several field trips they would like to take
- Which of several suggested topics they would like to study and in which order
- Which community service project they would like to adopt
- Which medium they choose for their artwork
- How they present their understanding of a topic in their project (straightforward oral reports, songs, poems, plays, videos, or visual displays)

Voice. Giving students a voice in the classroom, valuing what they have to say, is another tool for empowering them and thus for preventing anger from erupting. My colleague at the University of Georgia, Penny Oldfather, has coined the term *honored voice.* By listening to our students and caring about what they have to say, we help honor their voices (Oldfather, 1993). When we don't care about what students have to say, they feel dishonored, disrespected or "dissed" in their language. And what happens when students are dissed? They lash out in anger. Why? Because anger is the power they use to defend their wounded egos.

Does giving students a voice mean that they have the final say? Not at all. Rather, it means that we are willing to take their ideas into consideration:

- We will reflect about how we can incorporate subjects that are of interest to them.
- We will read their writings and respond thoughtfully.
- We will be sensitive to their expressions of feelings, be they positive or negative.

Yes, we'll honor their voices and listen to their ideas, but we teachers will still make the final decisions in our classrooms.

Responsibility. One of the greatest power tools we can give our students is responsibility. In her research of people who had suffered abuse as children, Zimrin (1986) examined the characteristics of those who had grown up to live normal lives and those who had dysfunctional adult lives. One of the critical variables Zimrin found was that most of the healthy survivors had to assume responsibilities during their childhood. Other major studies have confirmed that a strong sense of responsibility greatly enhances resilience (Werner & Smith, 1992). Responsibility gives people power in their lives. When we feel empowered, we are less likely to vent our rage destructively.

Required helpfulness (Rachman, 1979) is a strategy that many teachers have found to be successful for rechanneling behavior. Seven-year-old Toni was brought kicking and screaming into Ms. Bernard's first-grade classroom: "I hate school. I want to go home. Let me out of this damn place!" Toni had already attended two other schools where she had spent the bulk of her days in an isolated time-out room because of her violent outbursts and she had been retained one year. Imagine the nightmare for Ms. Bernard—having to cope with this child and the rest of her students as well. Unfortunately, many of us have been placed in similar quandaries.

Ms. Bernard adopted a required helpfulness plan as one of her strategies for acclimating Toni to her classroom. She arranged to pick up Toni in the front of the building 10 minutes before the rest of the students entered the classroom. Together, they walked to the class and chatted. In the classroom, Ms. Bernard assigned Toni some small tasks, for example, passing out paper, sharpening pencils, or erasing the board. Periodically during the day, she would also call on Toni for assistance. Toni felt needed and important—she felt empowered. This required helpfulness, coupled with Ms. Bernard's calm, caring approach, resulted in a miraculous behavior change for Toni within just a few weeks.

How can we send our worst discipline problems on errands? Who knows what trouble they'll get into outside of the classroom? Yet these are the very children who might benefit the most by being given responsibility. We can try to pair a child with behavior problems with another child who might be able to keep him or her in line and have them run an errand together. Sometimes we can't let a child out of our sight. If this is the case, we can try to enlist that child's help in the classroom. Passing out paper and other supplies, sharpening pencils, feeding the class pet, erasing blackboards, collecting papers, stapling material, designing bulletin boards, and setting up work areas are just a few examples of classroom responsibilities.

Working with a child's strength can be transformative for some children. Justin was a major disruptive force in the classroom. He was constantly making distracting noises that imitated bodily functions, inciting other classmates to act up, and picking fights in the playground. He seemed to have a chip on his shoulder. One day, Justin's science class began studying the sea. His eyes lit up. He was fascinated with fish and had read as many books as he could about them. He had even researched fish on the Internet and had communicated with a marine biologist. Justin's teacher seized this interest as an opportunity to enlist his required helpfulness. She asked Justin to prepare a lesson for the class and to be the resident expert to whom his classmates could come if they wanted some information about the sea. She also brought in an aquarium for the class and placed Justin in charge of maintenance and feeding. Soon, other teachers called on Justin for advice about their class fish. Justin no longer had the time or the need to attract negative attention.

Peer helper programs can also assist in transforming children's behavior by making the students feel needed. When an older child is asked to tutor a younger child, a weak student to help an even weaker student, or a charismatic troublemaker to be the class leader, the positive sense of power they acquire steers them away from rageful misbehavior. Community service is another avenue for helping children feel positive power. The KIDS Consortium is a nonprofit group that trains educators in integrating community service into students' academic work (see Resource B). Students who are channeling their energy into helping others are far less likely to be venting anger in our classrooms.

Beware of Power Struggles

One surefire way for everyone to get riled up is for teachers to get into a power struggle with students. As teachers, we feel that we need to be in control, yet, at the same time, our students are struggling to assert themselves and establish their own individual identity and status. If we back them up against the wall, they will lash back in anger either at that moment or at a later time. If we give them no graceful way to back out of a situation and maintain their dignity, they will come out shooting.

Billy's talking was getting on his teacher's nerves. "Get out in the hall this minute," Billy's teacher decreed. Billy remained seated. "Get out now." Billy remained seated. "Get out now or I'll carry you out." Billy remained seated. The teacher tried to physically remove Billy and Billy resisted and told his teacher to get his f____ hands off of him. All the children watched as the principal was called in to settle the ruckus. Who do you think lost?

Anger can be triggered by a sense of endangerment. If students feel trapped, if they feel there is no way to save face but to sacrifice their dignity and their image in front of others, they'll try to take control and lash back in anger. Although they may be punished, we will suffer as well. It's just not worth it. Instead, the teacher could have tried a variety of other approaches. Giving an I Message in a firm tone might have helped: "I get distracted when there is noise in the room and then it's hard for me to focus on what I am teaching"; "I am concerned when there is an undercurrent of talking, some children may not be able to hear"; or "I am worried that by talking, you may miss out on understanding this concept." Or the teacher could have directly said, "Billy, I realize that you may understand this already, but others don't and the talking can distract them and me"; or "Billy, please stop the talking, it's distracting." The teacher could have placed the responsibility onto Billy: "Billy, the talking is distracting. How can you help yourself not to do it?" (see Chapter 8 for further discussion of this problem-solving approach) or "Billy, please choose a place to sit where you won't be tempted to talk, because it's distracting." All these approaches get the message across very clearly and firmly that the behavior must be stopped without getting entangled in a power struggle.

Harnessing Our Own Anger

We're Human Too

I have yet to meet a teacher who didn't get angry sometime. We're human too! We are entitled to our feelings, including anger, just as our students are entitled to theirs. If we want to succeed in teaching our students to express their anger constructively, then we have to do the same. One way they learn is by copying us. For some children, we are their only adult model for appropriate behavior.

Pressures

We teachers are pressured from all directions—administrators, legislators, parents, the community, and children. Who wouldn't get angry and feel put-upon and overwhelmed at times! In this context, even normal children's behavior can sometimes infuriate us. We lose our cool because everything seems to be imploding on us. There are tests to grade, meetings to attend, lessons to plan, parents to assuage, administrators to please—we don't even have time to go to the bathroom! I have heard that teachers make up the bulk of urologists' patients. Is it any wonder? There's never a dull moment. Just when we think we have a minute to ourselves, something crops up. Under these conditions, it is understandable how, at times, we may lose our patience with our students, even when they have committed minor infractions or are only acting like children. Their behavior may be the straw that breaks the camel's back.

Frustrations

Times have changed. We seem to have so many more children in our classrooms nowadays with emotional and behavioral problems and learning disabilities. Many of our students' abilities to concentrate on their studies have been compromised by violence (real life and simulated), child abuse and neglect, and family disintegration. With so much else on their minds, it's hard for these students to concentrate. Sometimes when we teach these children, we receive blank stares, so we rephrase ourselves and we still receive blank stares. We try other methods and we receive yet more blank stares. Sometimes it seems nearly impossible to break through. Such frustration! We have feelings of helplessness and failure: "Why can't I make them obey?" "Why do they get to me so much?"

It's no wonder we feel angry! Although it is not the children's fault, it's not ours either. We cannot possibly be psychologists, social workers, and educators at the same time. Just as with children, our feelings of helplessness and powerlessness can make us angry.

Daily Hassles

Normal children's behavior can be infuriating at times. Why? Sometimes their behavior makes us afraid—for example, when they try dangerous tricks on the playground, we get angry because we're frightened; that's our primary feeling. When they fight, we often feel helpless and worried about someone getting hurt so we get angry. When we have a lot to do, deadlines to meet, and they move slowly, it raises our ire. When they daydream, it's annoying to have to repeat ourselves. Just because the behavior is normal doesn't mean that it won't get on our nerves. And normal children will misbehave. It goes with the territory of being a child. But just as it is normal for them to make mistakes sometimes, it's normal for us to feel annoyed and angry when they do.

Baggage From Our Private Lives

"Mom, where does Mrs. Lumpkin sleep at night? There's no bed in the school." Despite what some kindergartners may think, we all have lives beyond the classroom with our own responsibilities, joys, and worries. When we get in an argument with a loved one or are anxious about someone's health, it's hard to leave our feelings at the schoolhouse door. At those times, we can send out a clear alert to our students: "I'm feeling a bit stressed out today so tread carefully," "I'm upset about something today; it has nothing to do with you, but I am extremely sensitive"; or "I would appreciate extra cooperation today— I am not feeling well." Not only do communications like these help us get through the day, they help our students develop empathy, a critical aspect of emotional intelligence.

Baggage From Our Past

Sometimes, our students' behavior triggers painful memories of our own problems in school. The old adage "sticks and stones can break my bones but names can never harm me" is a big lie. Names can harm us and harm us deeply. Many of us still cringe at the mention of a name we were called in childhood. If we hear our students calling a student a hurtful name, we may explode, "Don't let me ever hear you call him a name again. How can you be so mean? If you say that again, I'll punish you. How would you like it if we called you that?" Our overreaction might very well make matters worse for the name-calling victim—now they might become "teacher's pet" or "baby." We should try to stop the name-calling while keeping our cool. Sometimes we may feel that our students are getting away with things that we never got away with. We may feel resentful and even a bit jealous.

We also bring our own cultural baggage with us. Behaviors that are perfectly normal in another culture may be foreign to us and even offensive. We may be furious when a child does not look at us when we are talking to him or her, because to us that seems disrespectful. However, in some cultures, it is considered disrespectful for a child to look an adult in the eye.

When we overreact, we can try to do some self-analysis: Why does this upset me so much? Does this remind me of something way back in my own childhood? We can try to remind ourselves, "Now is different. I am no longer a child. These children are not my family and my peers." Some teachers find it helpful to talk these kinds of situations through with a trusted colleague who isn't emotionally entangled. Understanding and then setting this childhood baggage aside can help us to stay calm during challenging discipline situations.

Harnessing Our Anger

Angry feelings in and of themselves aren't bad. It all depends on what one does with them. When expressed constructively and non-hurtfully, anger can be a terrific motivator for effecting change. Let's look at how we can harness our anger to effect positive change in our classrooms.

Step One: Notice Our Body's Message

"I was burning mad." "I was so angry my heart was beating a mile a minute." "I was so angry I felt like crying." "Every time I get angry I grind my teeth." Our bodies have marvelous ways of letting us know when we are angry and about to "lose it": feeling hot or cold, muscle tension, fist clenching, teeth grinding, sweating, laughing, crying, heart beating fast, head hurting, body shaking or shivering, body stiffness, twitching, or just frozen silence. By listening to our body's message we can become aware of our rising anger and harness it before it reaches a crescendo and gets out of control.

Step Two: Collect Ourselves

Once we hear our body signaling that we are about to lose it, we can try to collect ourselves. It is okay to let our students know that that's what we're doing:

1. Remove ourselves from the situation if possible. Perhaps we can stand in the hall by the door for a few minutes or call on a paraprofessional to take over for a short time. One teacher of young children sits in the rocking chair in her classroom, which she calls the "power chair." She tells the students that she's upset and needs to rock for a few minutes to collect herself. Not only does this help the teacher with her immediate dilemma, but it also models this behavior for her students.

2. Do deep breathing, count to 10, count backward from 10, or use visual imagery. Sometimes we can do this even when we're in the midst of teaching. It is okay for students to know what we're doing; they'll see that we have feelings, we're trying to express them constructively, and hopefully they will follow suit.

3. Do something with our hands—straighten the desk, write, or even put our hand up to our mouth to help us remember not to say anything we might later regret.

4. Physical exercise is a tremendous release but isn't possible when we are in the middle of teaching. Have you noticed that exercising each day helps take the edge off of things?

Step Three: Put It Into Words

Here's where an I Message can help us express our feelings in nonhurtful ways while getting our students to change their behavior. Keep in mind that our tone of voice as well as our words conveys our message. We need to be firm and direct to get our message across. If we smile while we're telling a student we're angry about something, the student will get a mixed message. Let's review the steps in constructing an I Message discussed in Chapter 4 and see how we can use it as a discipline tool.

"When . . ." Without accusing, we can describe the behavior we want changed. Being specific about the "when" (what was going on) provides students with clear information about what needs to be

changed and how they can do it, and it also encourages them to feel that they can indeed change and are not stuck in a rut. "You always . . ." or "You never . . ." implies that things are never going to change, although "Today . . ." or "I just noticed . . ." narrow it down to a manageable time frame.

It helps to limit ourselves to just this specific incident rather than bringing in all past infractions. If we stay focused on the issue at hand, students are less likely to tune us out like a broken record. What happens when we say, "If I've told you once, I've told you a hundred times. . . ."? They roll their eyes and think, "There she goes again."

The key here is also not to put the student on the defensive by pointing a finger with an accusatory "you." "I feel put-upon when there are papers on the floor" rather than "You're such slobs"; or "I feel distracted when there's an undercurrent of noise," rather than "You're such noisy people." It's highly unlikely that they will heed our words if they feel under attack and on the defensive.

"I Feel . . ." Here's where we try to put that primary feeling that lies below the anger into words—I feel worried, frustrated, hurt, overwhelmed, insulted, betrayed, frightened, disappointed, anxious, sad, concerned, or nervous. "I am worried that we will not finish our work if there are more interruptions." Students don't usually think about our feelings. In fact, they sometimes forget that we have any feelings. Some children are very sensitive when it comes to their own feelings but are not sensitive to the feelings of others. Here is yet another opportunity to develop their empathy for adults. And although our students may argue or disagree with our policies, they cannot argue with our feelings any more than we can argue with theirs. If we say "I'm disappointed that you misbehaved when I was out of the room," they can't say "No, you're not disappointed" or "No, you don't feel that way."

"Because . . ." This is when we explain why we feel this way, how their behavior tangibly and concretely affects us. We're not pulling our feelings out of thin air. We have a good reason for feeling that way. This sells our message because it justifies our right to our expectations. They see that it makes sense to expect the change: "I am concerned because we might not have enough time to play that kickball game today"; or "I am irritated because I cannot concentrate." What goes through our students' minds when they hear us talk this way? Typically, they might think "Gee, I had better hurry up so we can go out to play"; or "I had

better be quiet so the teacher can concentrate." Our "because" often causes them to stop and think about the ramifications of their actions and leaves the decision up to them.

Anger can motivate us to bring about change. By harnessing our anger and using I Messages, we teachers can use our anger to solve and even prevent some discipline problems. I Messages let students know how we feel, why we feel that way, and what they can do about it.

Summary of Main Points

❖ Both students and teachers are entitled to their angry feelings as well as to a variety of other feelings.

❖ We can defuse student anger by acknowledging their feelings, getting students to verbalize them, and guiding them to solve the problem that triggered the anger.

❖ Students and teachers can learn how to harness their anger and express it constructively.

❖ Some anger can be defused in the classroom by providing students with positive sources of power.

❖ The first step in harnessing anger is identifying when we are angry or when others are angry.

❖ The second step in harnessing anger is developing our own strategies for collecting ourselves.

❖ The third step in harnessing anger is talking directly and constructively in a nonblaming way.

6

What to Do After Students Misbehave

We all make mistakes, but everyone makes different mistakes.

—Ludwig van Beethoven

After all is said and done, no matter how well we organize our classrooms, no matter how clear our limits, and no matter how well we guide our students in positive directions, our students will still misbehave at times. Such is the nature of children. Our students are new at the game of life and, for a variety of reasons, they are bound to make mistakes.

Low-Key Discipline

Although student misbehavior usually calls for some sort of response on our behalf, fortunately, in most situations we don't have to do too much. We can do something low key to successfully nip the problem in the bud. Signaling, reminding, warning, ignoring, praising, and just stopping and doing nothing will work. We can call these tools for redirecting inappropriate behavior before it becomes a major disruptive factor in our classroom *low-key discipline*.

Signaling

Nonverbal. "The Look" can work miracles with some students. One good long hard stare from us and they settle right down. Eyes can be a very convenient silent discipline tool, and so can hands. Raising a finger to our lips as a signal for silence or pointing to the place in a text, or even using sign language to signal a command, can redirect a child without disrupting the flow of our lesson. In some cases, it is helpful to develop a special signal with a student who needs extra reminders to stay on track.

Verbal. "Cool it," "Let's keep a lid on it," and "It's time to settle down" are verbal signals that we can send to stop misbehavior in its tracks. I Messages can also signal to students the need for them to change their behavior: "I am concerned that with all the noise in the room we won't be able to finish our work on time"; or "I am worried that by passing notes you will miss out on important information."

Reminding

"DON'T LITTER" signs remind us of a rule we should already know. Every once in a while we all need reminders—especially children. Sometimes our students honestly forget rules or get so carried away that they lose sight of them. Just reminding a student about a rule may be enough to stop the misbehavior: "Remember, we need to bring our pencils and books to the group." "I hear talking. What should you be doing?" "Remind me about the rules for the playground." "Let's see how well we remember to walk down the hall."

Warning

Perhaps you can think back to how appreciative you were when a police officer gave you a warning rather than a ticket. You probably watched your speed after that (at least for a little while!). Sometimes a warning is just enough to get us back on track. Warning students what will happen if they do the same thing again may work at times. Just as we do, students often appreciate warnings: "The next time I see that toy on your desk I will have to take it away because it is distracting." Warnings work only if they are given once or twice. If we warn over and over again about the same thing, then our students will know that we don't really mean what we are saying. If a student still misbehaves after a warning, then we need to follow through with the consequences that we promised.

Have you noticed that sometimes we are more generous with our warnings to students who typically do not misbehave, and we often forget to give chronic misbehavers warnings but instead jump right into consequences. One of my student teachers reflected in her journal, "My supervising teacher gave many warnings to the 'better students' and no warning to the 'problem students.' The generally well-behaved kids got away with talking out of turn and shouting out answers, while the chronic misbehavers received checks or were asked to 'go back to your desk because you can't seem to control yourself on the floor with the rest of the class.' " All children have the potential for shaping up their behavior when given a warning, and chronic misbehavers deserve a chance as well.

Ignoring

Ignoring when a student is doing something minor and perhaps unintentionally wrong—for example, "not hearing" a cuss word that accidentally slips from the student's mouth, "not noticing" when students get into a little squabble, or "not seeing" a child's rising for a seventh-inning stretch—may be the best approach for us at times. Why not save our energy for bigger problems?

But ignoring small infractions is not the same as ignoring children who are seeking our attention. If a student is deliberately misbehaving to attract our attention, ignoring this misbehavior will probably result only in its escalation. After all, to a needy child, isn't negative attention better than no attention at all? The bottom line—ignoring small, perhaps unintentional mistakes—is sometimes a successful discipline strategy, but ignoring deliberate attention-getting misbehavior can backfire.

Praising

Isn't it human nature that when we are encouraged about something that we are doing, we will be more likely to do it again? Praising a student when he or she does something right even though at other times that student may do it wrong may inspire him or her to do the right thing more often: "You completed all the math problems correctly on today's homework assignment"; or "Your story is very interesting and well written."

Sometimes, when we see the positive, for example, a child who barely produces a few sentences and then one day writes an excellent story or the bully who torments others and then one day plays peacefully with another child, we may be tempted to comment: "Now that I see how well you wrote this, why can't you write like this every day?" or "You played cooperatively with the others today. Why can't you play that way with them all the time?" But doesn't this turn praise into chastisement or criticism? As such, it is unlikely to inspire positive change. Although certain forms of praise can positively redirect behavior at times, other kinds such as these are unlikely to inspire positive changes (see Chapter 3 for a further discussion of praise).

Doing Nothing

Sometimes if we just stop dead in our tracks, saying and doing nothing, the shock may remind students to shape up.

Discipline With a Capital D

As every teacher knows, low-key discipline does not work for all situations. At times, when students' misbehavior persists even after our low-key approach, we need to take stronger, more direct action to ensure that they don't repeat their offenses, such as fighting or being destructive. In this section, let's explore how insights into the causes of misbehavior and how setting consequences can help us deal with more major discipline problems.

Tracking Down the Causes of Misbehavior

Looking in the Mirror. Sometimes we can prevent future misbehavior by first figuring out why a student misbehaved and then making changes that will attack the problem at its source. The place to start with this approach is by looking in the mirror and asking ourselves:

• Is what I am asking my students to do worth doing? Is the task meaningful? If it's just busy work, why bother? If it's a time filler, why not let students pursue an interest of their own to fill the time? If students see no meaning in their tasks, they are less likely to become engaged in the learning process.

• Is what I am asking my students to do presented in an interesting fashion or does it just seem like drudgery? There are all sorts of ways to jazz up even routine tasks. Students can play Concentration to practice spelling words and learn multiplication tables by singing tunes. Variety is the key.

• Is what I am asking my students to do at the appropriate challenge level? If it's too easy, students will misbehave out of boredom, just to keep themselves occupied. If it's too hard, they might misbehave to distract us from their inability to learn. After all, isn't it more face saving to be labeled silly or annoying rather than stupid? Teaching to many different levels is indeed challenging, but it's even more challenging to deal with the constant hassles of discipline problems if we don't.

• Am I misreading cultural differences and interpreting them as misbehavior? In some cultures, it is disrespectful for a child to look an adult in the eye. Although we may assume that a student is being disrespectful when that child refuses to look us in the eye, even when we have told him or her to do so, the opposite may actually be the case. Touching others and minimizing personal distance is considered important in some cultures, yet we may assume that a student from one of these cultures is invasive and offensive. Some cultures are more boisterous than others. If we are from a less demonstrative culture, we may perceive their boisterousness as being threatening. Reading about cultures represented in our classrooms, seeing movies set in that culture, and talking to adult members of that culture, particularly our colleagues, can help us distinguish between cultural characteristics and deliberate misbehavior.

Keeping Anecdotal Records. If, in good conscience, we can be sure that our lessons are meaningful, interesting, and developmentally appropriate, then we can progress to examining misbehavior that originates with our students so that we can attack these problems at their source. Anecdotal records are most effective for gaining insight into the "why" behind a student's misbehavior. Jotting down who, what, when, where, and how can be enlightening.

- *Who:* Who are the players? Are other students involved? Which ones?
- *What:* What is the child doing or not doing that constitutes a problem? What seems to trigger the misbehavior?
- *When:* What time of day is it? After lunch? Before or after recess? Is it math time? Social studies time? Science time? Reading time? What events are happening in the class at the time? Before? After?
- *Where:* Where is this taking place? In the classroom? On the playground? During special activities?
- *How:* Specifically, how is the child behaving?

After keeping these records for several days, we may see patterns begin to emerge. If the behavior crops up right before lunch, low blood sugar may be the cause. If it's only during a particular subject, misbehavior may be a foil for feelings of inadequacy in that subject.

Understanding Common Causes of Misbehavior

Let's examine some of the more common causes of student misbehavior and what we can do to prevent these misbehaviors from occurring in the future.

Inexperience or Ignorance. On a goodwill visit, former President George Bush rode through the streets of Australia flashing a big grin and the "V" for victory sign. Unfortunately, his staff neglected to inform him that, in Australia, our victory sign is an obscene gesture. Did he deliberately intend to insult the Australians? Of course not. He simply did not know the rules of the land. Likewise, sometimes our students make mistakes and misbehave simply because they are novices in the game of life. Ignorance and inexperience lie at the base of their misbehavior. The young child who calls out his answers without raising his hand or who copies his neighbor's paper may not even realize he is doing something wrong. So, too, it is highly unlikely that the northern student transplanted to the south who neglects to say "Yes Ma'am" to her teacher is being intentionally rude. Doesn't it make sense to expect inexperience and ignorance from our students? Expecting it makes it easier to accept and prepare for it. What can we do about it? Making our rules very clear and explaining them with concrete examples can help relieve the ignorance: "We walk like this in the halls." "This is what an indoor voice sounds like. Let's practice." "When a new student arrives, this is how we can help that person feel comfortable." "When you bang into someone, say 'excuse me.' " Any time we start a new subject or venture out to a new place, we can review how we expect our students to behave: "When we use math manipulatives, we must keep them on the desks." "When we go on the field trip, you must stay together with your buddy." Also, practicing and role-playing new situations in advance can help avoid misbehavior that stems from ignorance or inexperience.

Physical Immaturity. Young children learn about the world by touching and by doing. Activity is their middle name. That's why it is so hard for many of them to sit still for more than a few minutes at a time. Their bodies, especially those of boys, are simply not yet settled enough to be still.

Even when they get older, our students' bodies may still take a while to slow down. Upper-elementary-age children's natural tendency is to run instead of walk and to reach out and touch instead of keeping their hands to themselves.

What can we do about it? Sometimes children simply cannot control their bodies. Sometimes it's easy for us to lose sight of the fact that we are expecting too much of our students, especially if we have taught a variety of grades. Reviewing child development texts or the NAEYC Developmentally Appropriate Guidelines (Bredekamp, 1987) can help refresh our memories so that we don't expect too much of our students. I have found it helpful to discuss student misbehavior with another colleague. When we realize that it's not just our students but all students their age who act that way, we may be able to be more tolerant of developmental characteristics.

Emotional Immaturity. Giggling and silliness are perfectly normal for 5- and 6-year-olds and perhaps even for older children. Yet this behavior certainly can disrupt a classroom. Daydreaming is also not uncommon in older elementary and middle school students. Although daydreaming may develop students' creative thinking abilities, their distraction from the tasks at hand can constitute a discipline problem for us.

What can we do about it? Just as with physical immaturity, we can read and talk with other teachers to be sure that our expectations of our students are on target. Sometimes, we must have to tolerate some of the normal developmental aspects of our students, including immaturity: "I can see you're feeling silly. You have 2 minutes to get it out of your system and settle down." "Your mind is wandering; try to put on your thinking cap." Other times we can guide them to more mature behavior: "I realize it may be hard not to laugh but that is not respectful, so keep it inside yourself."

Curiosity. We're all familiar with the *Curious George* stories. Poor Curious George. His curiosity created many problems for him and so many discipline problems for the man with the yellow hat. George didn't mean to press the fire alarm—he was just curious; he didn't mean to swallow the puzzle piece—he was just curious; he didn't mean to let the animals out of their cages—he was just curious. Likewise, the student who breaks the pencil may just be curious about what's inside rather than destructive. The student who keeps flipping through the pages of the book when told to turn to a particular page may not be deliberately defiant but just curious about what comes next. Normal curiosity may lead to misbehavior at times.

What can we do about it? Giving our students a few minutes to explore their books or play with their math manipulatives before they settle down to work lets them get their curiosity out of their systems so that they can then settle down to work: "You can flip through the book to see what's in it and then in 5 minutes we will begin the story on page 18." "You can play with the unifix cubes for 5 minutes. When the time is up, we will put them into rows of tens." If their curiosity results in their breaking something, then expecting them to repair the damage or to make restitution is perfectly reasonable.

Need for Belonging. Belonging and acceptance is a basic human need (Maslow, 1982). We all want to feel that we are part of a group. Sometimes students will act up just to gain the acceptance of others.

Some are defiant to prove that they are macho and to gain the awe of their peers. Some are cruel to others to prove their loyalty to a charismatic leader. Some use sneaky and underhanded behavior to gain acceptance. Many students will take whatever measures they deem necessary to become part of a group, even if it risks arousing the wrath of their teacher.

What can we do about it? There is much we can do to create a sense of community in our classrooms, where all students will feel accepted. First, it certainly helps when we are accepting of all students. We don't have to love all our students, but we can treat them all respectfully. All eyes are on us in the classroom. Students often guide their feelings about their peers according to what we think of their peers. Second, we can design experiences that can create group cohesion and acceptance, such as conducting class meetings, designing cooperative learning activities, and undertaking class community service projects. While they are working in groups, students can learn skills for successfully relating to others—for example, "When working together, one person will talk at a time." Third, when a child misbehaves while struggling for a sense of belonging, we can zero in on that child's special strength and call on him or her as a resource for the class. Becoming the "class expert" has opened the door to acceptance for many children.

Need for Recognition. "Ignore him. He's just looking for attention" is a common response to students who are annoying, loud, or disruptive in class. Yes, many students misbehave because they are starving for attention. They crave recognition. But as we discussed previously, ignoring them will only further exacerbate the problem; they will keep up their misbehavior until someone takes notice. After all, negative attention is much better than no attention at all, they think.

What can we do about it? We all need to feel important, that we matter, that we are noticed. Giving students responsibilities makes them feel important and recognized. Even if we cannot trust a child to run an errand on his or her own, we can pair that student with someone else to carry out the task. Many schools have found that delegating responsibility to chronic misbehavers can turn these children around 180 degrees. Examples are putting a child who defaced school property in charge of the grounds committee or training the class bully as the conflict mediator. Another way to help students feel important is to find a child's area of strength and let that child share his or her expertise with the class. Also, assigning important roles in plays and class performances to students whose misbehavior is a plea for recognition can be a sorely needed boost.

Need for Power/Control. Some children misbehave just to let us know who's in charge. Power and control is their goal. Ironically, children who come from two opposite family extremes, those who control their families and those who feel powerless in their families, often choose this route. Some who grow up in homes where abuse is unpredictable and random may deliberately misbehave just so they can predict and, therefore, control when they will be punished.

What can we do about it? Giving students choices from among acceptable options and allowing them to make certain decisions helps them feel that they have some control over their lives and that they are accepted and needed. In addition, problem solving is a terrific power tool. We can help them use problem solving to take control of their lives, responsibility for their actions, and to figure out how to make better choices (see Chapter 8).

Anger Release. Aggression is often triggered by angry feelings. Some students create discipline problems that are violent in nature because they are so full of anger and resentment, and they do not know how to handle their strong feelings or how to express their anger constructively. They lash out without thinking. They blow their stack, letting off steam to feel better, all the while making others in the classroom feel worse.

What can we do about it? We can help students become aware of what they are doing and to learn how to harness their anger and express it constructively. See Chapter 5 for a discussion on dealing with anger.

Although anger harnessing is important, it is learned over time. We also need an immediate response to children who lash out with mean words. Terri was furious because her teacher made her go to the end of the line for pushing. "Bitch," she spouted. "I don't want to hear that kind of language," responded her teacher, calmly but firmly; "I don't talk to you that way and I don't want to be treated that way either." See the first part of Chapter 5 for suggestions for dealing with anger on the spot.

Enjoyment, Adventure, and Fun. Sometimes students misbehave just because they are feeling their oats. They want to have fun. They're feeling silly and slap-happy and want to let it out. Irritating the teacher or another classmate can be exciting and entertaining.

What can we do about it? Consequenting this kind of behavior can be effective. Students must learn that they cannot do whatever they want just because they enjoy it. They must learn to act appropriately and to be accountable to others. In addition to making them aware of their behavior and consequenting their behavior, we can use problem solving as a tool to help them figure out how not to do the same thing again and what strategies they think will help them not disturb others even though they are sorely tempted. This kind of problem solving is discussed in detail in Chapter 8.

The following chart summarizes some of the "whys" of misbehavior and what we can do about it.

TABLE 6.1   The "Whys" of Misbehavior and the "Whats" We Can Do About It

Why Might This Student Be Misbehaving?	*What Can I Do About It?*
Inexperience or ignorance	Clearly, directly state expectations; demonstrate and practice appropriate behavior
Physical immaturity	Adjust expectations
Emotional immaturity	Adjust expectations; guide to mature actions
Curiosity	Free time to explore; require repairing damage
Need for belonging	Cooperative learning; involvement opportunities
Need for recognition	Responsibility; share expertise with class; acknowledgment of performance
Need for power or control	Choices; decisions, problem solving; responsibility
Anger release	Expression of feelings; anger harnessing practice, direct confrontation
Enjoyment, adventure, and fun	Awareness; consequences; problem solving

At times, we may find ourselves so beaten down by the misbehavior of one child or a group of children that we dread getting out of bed Monday through Friday. We're at wit's end, and we find it hard to be analytical and rational about the situation. Fortunately, we have a whole school full of resources that can help lift us out of our despair. Describing the situation and then discussing strategies with a neighboring teacher, a teacher who is our friend or mentor, a teacher who has taught these students in the past, the lead teacher, or the school counselor may provide relief. Organizing team meetings where teachers can present problems and the team suggests solutions can be invaluable. Teams consisting of an experienced teacher, the school counselor, and the principal, as well as those who have direct contact with students, such as a school bus driver or a cafeteria worker, can shed new light on the situation by pooling their knowledge. An excellent description of this collaborative approach to solving behavior problems can be found in Wolfgang and Glickman (1980).

Consequenting Misbehavior

In some cases, it is important for students to assume responsibility and make amends for their inappropriate behavior. That's where consequences come in. Four categories of consequences for teaching responsibility are restoration or restitution, composure, restriction, and reflection.

Restoration or Restitution. When someone breaks or loses someone else's property, whether it's intentional or not, the responsible, ethical thing to do is either to fix or restore the item to its original state if possible, or to make restitution. Therefore, the appropriate consequence for a student who breaks a classmate's pencil would be for him or her to replace it or to give the classmate money to buy another. The same goes for a student who bends a spoon in the cafeteria. If a student writes on a desk, then the consequence would be that he or she is required to clean it. The student who comes late to class is responsible for finding out about missed work. Enlisting parental support and working with parents to choose and carry out the consequence is important when we expect students to make restitution for lost or broken objects.

Composure. Sometimes when students get out of control, they need time and space to restore themselves, to collect themselves so that they can function civilly with others. That is where time-out as a consequence comes in. When a student "loses it," we can matter-of-factly and respectfully guide that student to a time-out area where he or she can read, write, draw, listen to music, rock on a rocking chair—whatever that student can do to restore his or her composure and rejoin the class.

Restriction. Sometimes, when students abuse privileges, an appropriate consequence is to restrict that privilege temporarily. If a student is not careful handling computer discs even after being given instructions, then restricting that student from using the computer makes sense.

Reflection. The most effective tool for preventing the repetition of misbehavior is to have a student reflect about the problem and figure out how he or she can prevent him- or herself from getting into the same situation again. Problem solving as a tool for student personal reflection will be explained in greater detail in Chapter 8.

Choosing a Consequence

Here are some questions I have found helpful to ask when choosing a consequence:

1. Does it make sense? Does it logically follow from what the student did? Is it related to the misbehavior?
2. Does it make the student accountable for his or her actions? Is the student responsible for correcting any damage or harm caused by the misbehavior? Is it a learning situation?
3. Above all, does it keep the child's and my dignity intact?

How Consequences Differ From Punishments

Some people might call this aspect of discipline punishment, but punishment differs from consequences in several ways.

Logical. Consequences flow logically from what the child did. They should be related to the misbehavior and make sense. Punishments are often not even connected to what the student did wrong.

Example: A student writes on a desk.
Consequence: The student must clean the desk.
Punishment: The student gets a check by his name and may
   miss recess as a result.

Example: A student cheats on a test.
Consequence: The student must take that test and possibly one
   or two future tests separated from the class.
Punishment: The student is sent to the office.

Child Accountable. Consequences make the child accountable for his or her behavior. They place the responsibility for correction in the hands of the student by requiring that the student correct the damage or harm caused by the misbehavior whenever possible or requiring that the student figure out alternative, acceptable behavior for him- or herself. Punishments place the responsibility for correction in the hands of the teacher.

Example: Two students are fighting.
Consequence: After cooling down, both students are required to
   sit down, discuss their problem, and work out a solution
   together.
Punishment: Both students are sent to the office to be paddled.

Example: A student does not complete her homework.
Consequence: The student must complete her homework dur-
   ing the class's free period.
Punishment: The child misses a field trip.

Dignity Intact. Consequences keep the child's dignity (as well as our own) intact. Punishments are often humiliating.

Example: A student cheats on a test.
Consequence: The teacher takes the student aside and has him
   complete a new test in private.

Punishment: The teacher yells at the child in front of the class, accusing him of being a cheater.

Example: A student takes money from the teacher's desk.
Consequence: The child must earn back the money to repay the teacher (perhaps at home or by doing odd jobs for the teacher at school).
Punishment: The child is accused in front of the class as being a thief and is made to apologize to the whole class.

Differentiating Between Consequences and Punishments

The same action can be a consequence or a punishment depending on the circumstances. Some discipline approaches use the word *consequences* for what are in reality *punishments,* perhaps because the word *consequence* doesn't sound so harsh or because they are trying to get the message across to the student that the punishment is a consequence of their action. But a rose by any other name is still a rose. If the approach is punitive rather than restorative, it's still a punishment. Let's look at how the very same action can be either a consequence or a punishment depending on the circumstances. We can use the above mentioned criteria of making sense, requiring student accountability and responsibility, and maintaining dignity to help us decide which category they fall into.

<u>*Time-Out as a Consequence:*</u> In these cases, time-out is used restoratively as a place where a student can go to restore and refresh him- or herself and to think about what should be done so that he or she can live peacefully in the classroom.

> Example A student begins to get very angry and to lose control. She is calmly but firmly told to go to time-out to collect herself before she does something that she will later regret.

> Example A student is constantly disrupting the class. He is sent to time-out to figure a plan of action for what he can do to help himself not be disruptive. He is to come back to the rest of the group when he regains his composure.

Time-Out as a Punishment: In these cases, time-out is meant to deliberately exclude a child from the reinforcement of the classroom with the logic being that by making it unpleasant, the child will not want to go back to time-out. This kind of time-out is often not logically connected to the child's infractions, originates in anger, and is meant to be punitive and to create discomfort for the child.

> *Example* A student does not complete his homework. He is sent to time-out.

> *Example* A student has three checks by her name—one for talking to a friend, one for not sitting still, and one for not taking her book out fast enough. Anyone who has three checks by his or her name for whatever reason must go to time-out.

Let's chart the uses of time-out based on our criteria for consequences:

TABLE 6.2   Evaluating Time-Out as a Consequence or as a Punishment

Action	Make Sense?	Student Responsibility?	Preserve Dignity?
To collect self	Yes	Yes	Yes
For plan of action	Yes	Yes	Yes
Because out of seat	No	No	No
Because incomplete homework	No	No	No

Loss of Recess as a Consequence: In these cases, the loss of recess time is logically connected to the child's misbehavior.

> *Example* A student who is playing roughly in the playground is required to sit out for the rest of recess.

> *Example* A student who consistently does not complete her homework is required to spend the first 5 minutes of recess attending to her homework.

Loss of Recess as a Punishment: In these cases, there is no logical relationship between the infraction and missing recess.

Example A student talks out in class and has to miss recess.

Example A student has four checks by his name—two for talking out of turn, one for running in the hall to the bathroom, and one for not turning in his work. Anybody who has four checks by his name misses recess.

Taking away recess as a punishment for misbehavior can be counterproductive. If a student has trouble sitting still and being quiet in class before recess, what happens to him after he or she has stayed still for all of recess? That student is most likely sitting there building up resentment. Without the opportunity to expend some of his or her energy during recess, chances are that the antsy behavior will be even worse after recess. In my opinion, recess is a basic necessity. Students need the physical exercise and informal social contact with their peers. As adults, we like breaks even when we attend 1½- to 2-hour lectures, yet we often expect young children to sit on their bottoms for 2 to 3 hours at a stretch without a break. In fact, evidence suggests that relaxation and exercise programs may directly improve behavior, social skills, and self-esteem, as well as academic performance (Knitzer, 1990).

In addition, some children become so obsessed and worried about whether or not they will miss recess that they do not pay attention in class. Having names on the board with checks can distract our students from the work at hand while they focus on their own personal tally.

TABLE 6.3 Evaluating Recess as a Consequence or as a Punishment

Action	Make Sense?	Student Responsibility?	Preserve Dignity?
Play roughly	Yes	Yes	Yes
Not complete homework	Sometimes	No	No
Talk in class	No	No	No
Four checks	No	No	No

Loss of Privileges. As a consequence, for example, a student who is sloppy with computer equipment and does not return disks to their proper location may lose computer privileges. As a punishment, a student who talks during silent reading loses computer privileges.

TABLE 6.4   Evaluating Loss of Privileges as a Consequence or as a Punishment

Action	Make Sense?	Student Responsibility?	Preserve Dignity?
No computer when sloppy with it	Yes	Yes	Yes
No computer when talk during silent reading	No	No	Yes

The bottom line is that consequences are appropriate for misbehavior when they enable students to assume responsibility for themselves. To use them as punishments to get back at students for misbehavior can be counterproductive.

Summary of Main Points

❖ Most misbehavior can be prevented but some cannot.

❖ There are times when just signaling, reminding, warning, ignoring, praising, or doing nothing will stop misbehavior.

❖ There are other times when a strong, direct approach to misbehavior is needed.

❖ Sometimes we can prevent future misbehavior by understanding the cause of the misbehavior.

❖ At times, students should experience consequences for their misbehavior.

❖ Consequences for misbehavior make sense, teach students to assume responsibility for their behavior, and preserve the student's and the teacher's dignity.

7

Problem Solving as a Tool for Teachers

In the middle of difficulty lies opportunity.
—Albert Einstein

What makes discipline so challenging is that misbehavior is such a complicated issue. Students misbehave for all sorts of reasons and in all sorts of ways. It sure would be convenient to find one answer that would work all of the time, but a "one-size-fits-all" solution simply does not exist. Fortunately, however, there is a skill we can call on to help us find the answers: problem solving. Problem solving can be a terrific vehicle for determining our course of action when it comes to discipline issues.

As teachers, we are already familiar with the value of problem solving for figuring out math problems, for examining history, and for conducting scientific experiments, for example. We can take our knowledge of this process and apply it to discipline as well. First, let's explore how we can use the problem-solving process to help us figure out what caused the misbehavior, how we can prevent future problems, and how we can select appropriate consequences. Then, in the next chapter, we will examine how we can guide our students to use the problem-solving process to figure out how to replace inappropriate behavior with appropriate behavior and how to resolve their conflicts with each other. Keep in mind that, at first, this process may be awkward and time-consuming for us and our students but, with practice, the thought patterns will soon become automatic.

Problem-Solving Steps

Before we apply them to discipline, let's review the general structure of the problem-solving steps:

1. *State the problem.* Before figuring out a solution, problem solvers have to know what the problem is. Summarizing the problem in one or two sentences is helpful.
2. *Brainstorm ideas.* Coming up with as many ideas for solving the problem as possible and recording them is the goal of this step. Quantity of ideas, not quality, is what counts. One idea leads to another. A bad idea may lead to a good idea.
3. *Evaluate ideas.* Each idea from Step 2 is carefully examined to determine whether it will work and why it will or why it will not work.
4. *Select a mutually acceptable idea.* The key is to find an idea that is acceptable to all parties concerned and that will work best to solve the problem stated in Step 1.
5. *Try out the idea.* The solution chosen in the previous step is implemented.
6. *Evaluate effectiveness.* It is critical to determine whether the chosen solution works. Does it solve the problem described in Step 1?
7. *Decide.* If the answer to Step 6 is yes, and the solution solves the problem, mission accomplished. If, however, the answer is no, the problem solvers can either (a) return to Step 4 and choose another solution, (b) return to Step 2 to design more solutions, or (c) return to Step 1 to be sure they put their finger on the real problem. The key is to persist until the problem is solved.

Problem Solving as a
Discipline Tool for Teachers

We can use problem solving to help us figure out why a student is misbehaving, figure out what we can do about the "why," and select appropriate consequences for misbehavior if necessary. Let's look at some classroom examples that show how we can use problem solving to figure out what to do when our students misbehave: why they are misbehaving, what we can do to prevent the misbehavior, and what consequences are appropriate. We will go through each of the problem-solving steps slowly. Of course, we don't have the luxury of time in the heat of the moment in the classroom but, with practice, thinking these steps through will become automatic and speedy.

Figuring Out Why a Student Is Misbehaving

> Example Kindergarten student Tim has been told repeatedly to sit on his name tape during group time. Nevertheless, he continues to get up and walk around the room, bumping into other children.

We need to use only the first four problem-solving steps to identify the source of the problem, or why it happened.

1. *State the problem.* The teacher asks herself, "Why does Tim persist in moving around and disturbing others?"
2. *Brainstorm ideas.* This is the step where she tries to think of as many ideas as she can for why Tim is wiggling around: "He is trying to get on my nerves." "He's a poor listener." "He's spoiled and is used to doing whatever he wants to." "He is physically immature and his body can't keep still." "He's bored." "He's uncomfortable."
3. *Evaluate ideas.* Now is the time for the teacher to go through each idea on the list to see what she thinks of it.
   • Trying to get on nerves: "Tim is usually a very sweet child. He's very polite. I don't think he's being deliberate."
   • Poor listener: "Tim can repeat stories we read word for word so I know he listens."

- Spoiled: "Tim doesn't seem any more indulged than any of the other children in class."
- Physically immature: "Tim is very active all of the time, in class and out. He always likes to keep moving. Maybe he is physically unable to sit still."
- Bored: "I try to keep things moving so children won't be bored. He doesn't seem bored."
- Uncomfortable: "He may be uncomfortable. It can be awkward to sit on the floor."

4. *Select an idea.* The teacher decides, "I think the problem is that Tim simply can't sit still for very long. He seems to have an inborn moving mechanism." (In this case, for the sake of demonstration, we are assuming that this is the problem. In other situations, you may find that there is a different source for the problem.)

Example Sara, a fourth grader who has a short fuse and often seems angry or negative, broke the calculator that was on the teacher's desk.

1. *State the problem.* The teacher asks himself, "Why did Sara break the calculator?"

2. *Brainstorm reasons.* The teacher generates possible reasons for Sara breaking the calculator: "She wanted to see how it works and it broke as she was using it." "She was angry at me and tried to get back at me by breaking the calculator." "Maybe she was pushing the buttons too fast and too strongly." "Maybe she tried to take it to her desk and she dropped it."

3. *Evaluate ideas.* Now the teacher goes through each possibility to see what he thinks of it.

- Curiosity: "She had used it many times and was familiar with it. I don't think she was just curious."
- Anger: "Right before that happened, I had reprimanded Sara for something. She has a bad temper."
- Carelessness: "She knows how to push the buttons. She's usually pretty careful with things."
- Clumsiness: "I didn't notice her dropping it."

4. *Select an idea.* The teacher decides, "I think Sara was trying to get back at me for reprimanding her."

Even in a situation such as this one where the child might have been vengeful, it is important to brainstorm other possible reasons before we take action to be sure that we don't jump to unfair conclusions. Sometimes, especially with chronic misbehavers, we may automatically assume the worst of them. Brainstorming helps us to avoid doing this.

Figuring Out What to Do About the Why

Now let's look at these same two examples and use problem solving to help us figure out what to do to prevent these problems from occurring in the future.

> Example Kindergarten student Tim has been told repeatedly to sit on his name tape during group time. Nevertheless, he continues to get up and walk around, bumping into other children because he is physically unable to stay still.

Now that the teacher thinks she knows the source of Tim's problem, it's time for her to figure out what she can do to prevent the problem from happening again by attacking it at the source. This time she can use all seven problem-solving steps.

1. *State the problem.* She asks herself, "How can I prevent Tim from moving around and disturbing others during group time, knowing that he has a hard time staying still?
2. *Brainstorm ideas.* She comes up with several possible solutions to this problem: "I could eliminate group time." "I could give Tim a special space where he would have more room to move." "I could put him in time-out." "I could give him a stopwatch and see if he can sit still for a short period of time. I could gradually increase the sitting-still time."
3. *Evaluate ideas.*
   - Eliminate group time: "Group time is important. I am not willing to give it up for one child."

- Give Tim a special space: "This could work. I could explain to him where his space would be and how it could help him."
- Time-out: "Tim will miss out on the work that we are doing."
- Stopwatch: "This might work. It would keep him focused, and he could gradually build up his endurance. However, he may not be physically able to sit still no matter how hard he tries."

4. *Select an idea.* The teacher decides, "I'll work with Tim to find a special space for him."

5. *Try out the idea.* Together with Tim, the teacher finds a special place for him near the group but with enough moving room so that he does not disturb anyone else.

6. *Evaluate effectiveness.* The teacher notices to her delight that Tim isn't disturbing anyone anymore.

7. *Decide.* Because he's not disturbing anyone, the problem is solved.

If Tim had kept on disturbing people, the teacher could go back to determining the reasons and look for other possible explanations for his behavior, or she could choose another solution, such as using a stopwatch, to help him gain some control.

> Example Sara, a fourth grader who has a short fuse and often seems to be angry or negative, broke the calculator that was on the teacher's desk because she was angry at the teacher.

1. *State the problem.* The teacher asks himself, "How can I help Sara learn to manage her anger so that she does not lash out destructively?"

2. *Brainstorm solutions.* The teacher generates several possible solutions to the problem: "I could send her to the school counselor." "I could take her aside and teach her alternative ways to express her anger." "I could punish her when she lashes out." "I could send her to time-out."

3. *Evaluate solutions.* The teacher examines all the solutions she came up with in Step 2.

- Counselor: "She really does need individual help. I'll refer her to the school counselor."
- Take aside: "I can try to find some time to teach her some cooling-down strategies. I'll also set aside time to listen to her feelings, perhaps during recess or lunch, so that she can get her feelings out and I can help her deal with them constructively."
- Punish: "She'll probably just get angrier."
- Time-out: "Sometimes when she goes to time-out she gets even angrier."

4. *Try out solution.* The teacher decides, "I'll refer her to the counselor and I'll also try to notice when she's getting worked up, make her aware of what's happening, and help her develop some cooling-down strategies."

5. *Evaluate solution.* The teacher notices that "Sara seems to be more comfortable in the classroom and is less angry."

6. *Decide.* The teacher concludes, "The counselor and I seem to be teaming well to help Sara. We'll keep it up. If Sara's angry posture persists, it might be helpful to encourage her parents to seek professional help for her."

The teacher might also seize this opportunity to reflect on his relationship with Sara. Could he have reprimanded Sara in such a way that embarrassed her? Can he take special care with his tone and words with such a sensitive child?

Determining the Consequences for Misbehavior

Example Kindergarten student Tim has been told repeatedly to sit on his name tape during group time. Nevertheless, he continues to walk around, bumping into other children because his body seems too immature to stay still.

In this situation, there is no need to brainstorm a separate consequence for Tim's behavior. The approach taken by the teacher of adjusting her seating demands should solve the problem for the moment and prevent it from happening in the future. Consequences are not necessary for every misbehavior. Sometimes, as in this case, we can restructure the environment to solve the problem.

In the case of Sara, however, figuring out a consequence would be the next appropriate step because she should be held accountable for her deliberate misbehavior.

> Example Sara, a fourth grader who has a short fuse and often seems to be angry or negative, broke the calculator that was on the teacher's desk.

1. *State the problem.* "How can I consequent Sara for breaking the calculator?"
2. *Brainstorm ideas.* "I could yell at her and let her know how furious I am." "I could send her to time-out to think about what she did." "With her parents' permission, I could expect her to do extra work to earn money to pay for the calculator." "I could forbid her from going near my desk." "I could contact her parents and let them know what she did."
3. *Evaluate ideas.*
   - Yell: "Yelling will only help me to let out my tension and anger. It probably won't stop her from doing the same thing again. It will also model poor self-control for a child who already has poor self-control and she may even enjoy getting that reaction from me."
   - Time-out: "She may not even realize what's so wrong about what she did. She may sit in time-out and justify her actions or just get angrier and more resentful."
   - Extra work: "This will teach her responsibility for her actions and I'll be able to replace the calculator. I'll contact her parents and together, Sara, her parents, and I can work out how she will earn money to pay for it."
   - Forbid from desk: "This isn't realistic. Students need to approach my desk at times and, besides, I can't monitor her all the time."
   - Contact parents: "This might undermine my authority if I ask them to do something about Sara's behavior, and I am not sure how her parents will react."

Let's chart our solutions, using the criteria that we established in Chapter 6 for consequences:

TABLE 7.1   Evaluating Solutions for Misbehavior

Action	Make Sense?	Student Responsibility?	Preserve Dignity?
Yell	No	No	No
Time-out	No	No	Maybe
Extra work	Yes	Yes	Yes
Desk ban	Maybe	No	No
Anger harness	Yes	Yes	Yes
Contact parents	Maybe	No	Maybe

4. *Select an idea.* Having her do extra work to pay for what she broke meets our criteria for consequences and is the solution that is most likely to prevent the same behavior from recurring.

5. *Try out the idea.* Depending on the child's home circumstances, the teacher, the parents, and the student could work out a plan for her to earn the cost of the calculator. Perhaps she could do extra chores at school or at home.

6. *Evaluate effectiveness.* If the teacher notices a gradual improvement in Sara's behavior, for example, fewer angry outbursts, then he will know that she is heading in the right direction. Rome was not built in a day. We can't expect miraculous behavioral changes overnight. In fact, often it is wise for us to beware of miracle behavior changes—those are usually the shortest lasting.

If the teacher notices some improvement, she can keep it up. The consequence alone might not stop the misbehavior. If no improvement is noticed, the teacher can try to figure out other ways to help Sara with her low frustration level.

An additional step is warranted in this situation. Sara should be asked to reflect on how she can help herself find alternative ways to express her anger so that she does not lash out physically or verbally when she is angry. We will discuss this student version of problem solving in Chapter 8.

More About Problem Solving for Consequences

Let's further examine how we can use problem solving to choose appropriate consequences for misbehavior. Sometimes we may be so furious about the student's misbehavior that we overreact and want to enforce every consequence we can think of—have them miss recess, miss a party, yell at them, and so forth. But this approach undermines our effectiveness. One well-thought-out consequence is far better than several impulsive ones. Let's keep in mind the criteria for choosing a consequence discussed in Chapter 6; namely, Does it make sense? Does it involve the child in assuming responsibility? Does it preserve the child's and my dignity?

Example A student skips school.

1. *State the problem.* "What would be an appropriate consequence for skipping school?"
2. *Brainstorm ideas.* "In-house suspension." "Writing 100 times, 'I must not skip school.' " "Make up the work missed after class." "Suspension from school."
3. *Evaluate ideas.*
   - In-house suspension: "The student will miss more class work and may fall even further behind. This may create more work for me in the long run."
   - Write 100 times: "The student won't learn anything from this. It's really just a waste of time. Besides, it sends the message that writing is meaningless and that school work is unpleasant."
   - Make up work: "This way I give the student the message that our work is important. If he has to make it up, he's less likely to skip again."
   - Suspension: "This might actually be a reward for the student—he gets two days off from school for the price of one!"

Table 7.2   Evaluating Solutions for Misbehavior

Action	Make Sense?	Student Responsibility?	Preserve Dignity?
In-house	No	No	Maybe
Write	No	No	Maybe
Make up work	Yes	Yes	Yes
Suspension	No	No	No

4. *Select an idea.* "I will require the student to make up the work after class."

5. *Try out the idea.* The teacher gives the student the work missed with a deadline for turning it in.

6. *Evaluate its effectiveness.* "The student hasn't skipped school since."

7. *Decide.* The problem seems to be solved. Skipping school may have seemed like fun, but it surely wasn't worth all the work afterward. If the student is still skipping school, it might be important to try to use problem solving for figuring out the reason for the skipping. Perhaps the student is feeling discouraged, depressed, caught up with a gang, or is having family problems.

Example   A student rips down a class banner.

1. *State the problem.* "What would be an appropriate consequence for ripping down the class banner?"

2. *Brainstorm solutions.* "Time-out." "Miss recess." "Rehang the banner." "Student must call parents and explain what she did."

3. *Evaluate solutions.*

   • Time-out: The student may be removed from our eyesight (understandably, we may be so angry that we'd like her to disappear) and kept from socializing with her peers, but the banner still remains down.

   • Miss recess: This may be upsetting to the child, but only temporarily. She may not understand the connection between recess and the banner and, besides, children need recess to let out their energy and get some exercise.

- Rehang the banner: By hanging the banner, the child assumes responsibility for her actions. If it's a challenge to rehang, it is unlikely that she'd rip it down again.
- Call parents: We undermine our authority when we rely on parents to discipline their children for problems that occur in school. (This is different from problem solving with parents discussed in the Introduction.) Although it's best to inform parents when serious incidents occur, we may not choose to do so if we fear the home consequences for the child.

TABLE 7.3 Evaluating Solutions for Misbehavior

Action	Make Sense?	Student Responsibility?	Preserve Dignity?
Time-out	Yes	No	No
Miss recess	No	No	No
Rehang banner	Yes	Yes	Yes
Call parents	No	No	No

4. *Select a solution.* "I'll require the child to hang the banner. I'll have to stand behind her on the ladder to be sure she is safe."
5. *Evaluate the solution.* The banner has not come down again.
6. *Decide.* Because the banner remained up, the problem is solved. If the banner had remained up, but the child was destructive with other school property, then it would be wise to start out by using problem solving to figure out the cause of this destructive behavior. Putting our heads together with the school counselor and principal is often beneficial in getting to the core of the destructive behavior.

You may be wondering, "What teacher could possibly have the time to go slowly through all these problem-solving steps?" Relax. With practice, problem solving becomes second nature and comes nearly automatically. Many teachers have found that it is well worth the initial effort to get it going because it is a discipline technique that really works, and one that de-escalates rather than escalates problems.

Summary of Main Points

❖ Problem solving is a tool that teachers can use to decide how to deal with misbehavior.

❖ Teachers can use problem solving to help them figure out why a student is misbehaving.

❖ Teachers can use problem solving to help them figure out what to do about the "why" of the misbehavior.

❖ Teachers can use problem solving to determine appropriate consequences for misbehavior.

8

Problem Solving as a Tool for Students

The ultimate aim of education is the creation of the power of self-control.

—John Dewey

Students can use problem solving to figure out how they can assume responsibility for replacing their inappropriate behavior with appropriate behavior. We can refer to this form of problem solving as social problem solving because it is a social process—we are interacting with students, teaching them how to problem solve with us and with others, and teaching them how to solve social (behavioral) problems.

By guiding the students to figuring out what they can do, rather than threatening them about what we will do, we help them develop responsibility for their own behavior. The burden is placed on the student rather than on us to change the behavior, and the student is more likely to take ownership of the solution. If a child bothers his or her neighbors and we move that student to another seat, the burden for changing the behavior falls on us. Chances are that student will find some other way to distract his or her peers. But if, instead, we ask the child how he or she can help figure out a way not to disturb his or her peers, that student may very well suggest moving seats. Changing the behavior becomes the student's responsibility. Because the student chose the solution, he or she will be more likely to ensure that it works.

Just as we can effectively use problem solving as a discipline tool to help us reflect about student misbehavior and what we can do about it, so too can we teach our students to use problem solving as a discipline tool to help themselves reflect about how they can exercise self-control when it comes to their own behavior. A considerable body of research shows that children even as young as 4 years old can be taught how to problem solve (Spivack, Platt, & Shure, 1976; Thornton, 1995). The ability to solve problems does not seem to depend on being very smart or being able to engage in abstract reasoning. Factual knowledge about the problem domain, not sophisticated logic, determines how successfully a child can address a problem (Thornton, 1995). If children are given feedback about their actions and information about the situation and their options, they can gain insight that will allow them to develop problem-solving strategies, whether they are preschoolers or high schoolers, gifted or of average intelligence.

The Benefits of Problem Solving for Students

Teaching students social problem solving provides terrific benefits. In addition to noting social benefits, such as improved social adjustment, less vandalism, and less aggression (Elias & Clabby, 1992), teachers have found that there is a positive spillover to academic performance. They spend less time helping students with academic as well as social and emotional problems. All of the following byproducts of problem solving, including hope, optimism, and self-efficacy, have been positively correlated to academic success.

Hope

Problem solving teaches students hope—the belief that they have both the will and the way to accomplish their goals, whatever those goals may be (Snyder, Harris, Anderson, & Holleran, 1991). In a study

comparing the academic achievement of students who were]
low on hope, researchers found that hope is a better predictor of
than the S.A.T. Students who had high hope had higher goals ×
worked harder to attain them (Snyder et al., 1991). By looking at a
problem, brainstorming solutions, and choosing a solution that will
enable them to reach their goal, students see that there is hope for a
positive resolution of their problems.

Optimism

Optimistic people consider failure to be due to something that
can be changed. With effort, they feel that they can succeed the next
time. Pessimistic people ascribe failure to long-lasting personal characteristics and feel that they are helpless to change (Seligman, 1995).
All of us know the frustration and pain of working with a pessimistic
child who thinks, "I'll never be able to do it," or "There's nothing I
can do." Problem solving can lead to optimism. If students have a
problem, they can be encouraged by knowing that they can follow the
steps and try to find a solution. Although the first solution may not
work, students know that they can go back and try to find another
solution until they succeed. With problem solving, there's a light at
the end of the tunnel.

Self-Efficacy

Underlying hope and optimism is the belief that one can have
mastery over one's own life and can meet challenges as they come up
(Goleman, 1995). Problem solving is a mastery tool. Students can
figure out how to master situations on their own and how to bounce
back from failures.

Teaching Our Students Problem Solving

In order for our students to learn how to problem solve, we have to
teach it to them. The best way to accomplish that goal is by modeling
the problem-solving process for our students, integrating problem
solving into the curriculum, and guiding students through the process
until they have mastered the skill.

Modeling

Why not talk it through aloud when we engage in the problem-solving process? "Let's see, how can I be sure that we don't lose track of time and are not late for lunch? I could set my timer. Tim could remind me . . ." "I wonder where I can set up this science center? By the cabinets, by the window, in the far corner? By the cabinets, we can't reach them; near the window may be too cold; the far corner will work . . ."

Integrating Into Curriculum

Using problem solving as a model for discussing books that the class is reading can help students better understand this skill and give them practice using it. "The problem for the billy goats was how to get over the bridge with the troll. What were their solutions? What other solutions can you think of?" Problem solving can also be used as a model for tackling math problems, for example, "How do you think we can solve this problem? What would happen if we tried this?" and for conducting science experiments, "Why do you think this happened? What could we do if we didn't want this to happen?" Problem solving can be seamlessly woven into what we are already doing. We can take our current curriculum content and approach it from a problem-solving perspective.

Guiding

It is helpful to go through all of the problem-solving steps with students when they are first learning the process. We can help them state the problem by asking questions and enlightening them as to the situation. We can brainstorm together with them, contributing our ideas as well as encouraging them to contribute theirs. We can discuss with them the consequences of selecting each idea that they have mentioned. We can encourage them to make their own decisions based on these discussions and then support their decisions.

Learning how to problem solve is a social process for children. Students can learn problem-solving skills through *guided participation,* a collaborative process whereby an adult and a child share a problem, the adult explains and supports the child's efforts, and both the child and the adult are involved in the process of making the decision (Spivack & Shure, 1975, p. 148). We adults provide the scaffolding, as the Russian psychologist L. S. Vygotsky (1962/1986) explains; we support the child's efforts, explain ideas, and encourage the child to stretch. According to Vygotsky, students can learn problem solving in the context of everyday activities through their social interactions with us adults.

This may seem like just one more teaching burden when we already feel stretched to the limit. Initially we will have to put in more time to teach problem solving because students learn it best with our direct guidance or scaffolding. But the beauty of the system is that, as time goes on, we'll have to provide less and less scaffolding. Teachers throughout the United States have found that after the initial teaching phase, their load is actually lightened. It is amazing how quickly students begin to learn to think for themselves and to make wiser decisions on their own. Our job gets easier as they learn self-control and responsibility for their own behavior.

What Students Learn From Social Problem Solving

Each of the problem-solving steps teaches our students critical life skills.

1. *State the problem.* Often students aren't even aware of the problem that their behavior may be creating. This may be the case with a student who hums absent-mindedly to herself. Other times, they are fully aware of what they are doing but are unaware of its effect on others, such as the student whose nervous tapping distracts those around him. Some may not realize until we point out how their feelings and actions are influenced by the feelings and actions of others—how they can get "hooked" into misbehaving. At this beginning step of problem solving, we can heighten our students' awareness and sensitivity to the nature and causes of the problem.

2. *Brainstorm solutions.* Often children see no other path than the one they are taking, such as the child who sees hitting as the only option when he or she is insulted. Through brainstorming, we can

open their eyes to other options and they can develop the capacity to generate a variety of alternative solutions to a problem.

3. *Evaluate solutions.* Many students don't think beyond what they are doing and the pleasure it may bring them. They don't think of the effects of their actions on others, such as the child who keeps tapping on his desk. By discussing each of the solutions brainstormed in Step 2 and evaluating the ramifications of each, students learn to consider the consequences of their actions. They also learn empathy as they discuss how other people might respond to each solution that they are evaluating.

4. *Select a mutually acceptable solution.* By working to find an idea mutually acceptable to all parties concerned, students learn the art of give-and-take and, consequently, the art of compromise.

5. *Try out the solution.* After students have chosen a solution, we can help them articulate, step by step, how they will carry out the solution. Some children have no idea how to proceed to change. Specifying the details, step by step, gives them a map to guide themselves and teaches them how to plan in the future.

As we teach them problem solving, we can help our students understand why "I promise I'll never do it again" or "I'll be good" are unacceptable solutions. These are empty words with no actions planned to back them up. Students need to have a plan of action for carrying out the solution. They need to choose exactly what appropriate behaviors they will use to replace inappropriate behaviors.

6. *Evaluate the solution.* By discussing with students how well they think their solution is working, we are teaching them to be reflective about their actions.

7. *Decide.* The most critical piece of information that students learn from this step is that if they don't succeed at first, try and try again. Although this solution did not work out, another might. This is a message of hope and accountability. Even if they mess up, they can go back and figure out another solution to the problem (Spivack et al., 1976).

Examples of Social Problem Solving

Let's look at this social problem-solving process in action.

Example Sara, a fourth grader, broke the calculator that was on the teacher's desk because she was angry at the teacher.

1. *State the problem.* "I can see that you were very angry, Sara. What can you do the next time you are angry that will help you express your anger without lashing out hurtfully at people or property?"

2. *Brainstorm solutions.*

   Sara: I'll just stop.

   Teacher: Let's try to find a specific plan.

   Sara: I'll go somewhere and scream.

   Teacher: What else could you do?

   Sara: I could rock in the rocking chair.

   Teacher: Anything else?

   Sara: I could come and tell you.

   Teacher: Maybe you could write down how you're feeling.

   Sara: I could draw or scribble and then rip it up.

3. *Evaluate solutions.*
   - Just stop.
     Teacher: That's not a plan. It's hard to just stop without knowing what to do instead.
   - Go somewhere and scream.
     Teacher: There may be nowhere to go. Besides, it might disturb others.
   - Rocking chair.
     Sara: I don't like that rocking chair.
   - Tell teacher.
     Sara: Maybe. That might work if you can help me.
   - Write feelings.
     Sara: That's too much bother.

- Draw or scribble.

    Sara: I like to draw; that might help me.

4. *Select a solution.*

    Teacher: Sara, would you like to come and tell me when you are upset or would you like to go somewhere and draw?

    Sara: Can I do both?

    Teacher: Sure. I'll save a special pack of crayons and a pad of paper in my desk drawer. When you start to get very angry, come and tell me and I'll help you settle down. You can also go to that desk drawer and take out the crayons and paper.

5. *Evaluate solution.* Sara began to tell her teacher when she was feeling very angry. Sometimes she drew and then ripped up her paper. After a couple of lapses, she stopped her destructive behavior.

6. *Decide.* The problem is solved. If Sara had continued to lash out, then Sara and her teacher could go back to Step 2 or 3. A child this angry might also benefit from individual counseling where she could get at the root of her problem.

Example Serena is constantly chatting with her classroom neighbors, regardless of where she is sitting.

1. *State the problem*

    Teacher: Serena, I notice that you like talking to your neighbors during class. I get distracted when there is noise in the class and I worry that other students won't be able to hear important information (I Message). I wonder what you could do to help yourself not talk so much during class.

Notice that the teacher says, "I wonder what *you* could do . . . to *help yourself,*" which is a clear message that self-control is the desired outcome.

2. *Brainstorm ideas.* The teacher and Serena each contribute ideas, with one of them writing the ideas down as they go along so that there is one common list.

Serena: Move me away from the others.

Serena: I'll try to remember but if not, give me a reminder.

Teacher: Perhaps you could put your hand near your mouth to remind you.

Serena: How about if I write down what I feel like saying?

In brainstorming, no one individual takes credit for an idea, and therefore, the ideas become communal property. Because Serena and the teacher brainstormed together, they will both feel ownership of the solutions and develop camaraderie in the process.

3. *Evaluate ideas.* Together Serena and the teacher consider each option.
   - Move away.
     Serena: I don't like to be isolated from everyone else. It embarrasses me and I feel lonely.
     Teacher: I understand. It feels awkward to me too.
   - Reminder.
     Serena: I forget myself and get carried away. Maybe if you gave me a signal, I could catch myself.
   - Hand to mouth.
     Serena: I don't think I'll remember to do that. Besides, it's awkward if I'm writing.
   - Write.
     Serena: I suppose I could write it down, but that would be boring.
4. *Select a solution.* Serena decided that she liked the idea of a signal best. Together she and her teacher planned the signal. The teacher would tap twice on her cheek if she noticed Serena talking.

If we decide what to do single-handedly without such a discussion, we are placing the burden of enforcement on ourselves and the student is not learning self-control. If, however, the student is included and decides together with us what might help her control her own behavior, she will own the solution and be more likely to stick to it.

5. *Try out the solution.* The teacher tapped twice on her cheek when she noticed Serena talking. Serena enjoyed the private signal, the opportunity to please her teacher, and to feel good about her own self-control. Her talking episodes became fewer and shorter.

6. *Decide.* After a week, Serena and her teacher discussed how their signal was working. They both agreed that Serena still talked some, but she was definitely talking less. The signal seemed to be working so they decided to keep it up.

As we mentioned before, we can't expect miraculous behavior changes overnight. Although the talking was not extinguished, Serena was heading on the right path and that's what counts. If the talking was still a problem, then Serena and her teacher would have had to go back and find another solution. Perhaps they would return to Step 2 and brainstorm more ideas, or just go to Step 3 and select one of the previously mentioned solutions. In either case, they would not give up until the problem was solved.

Example Andy uses profanity when he gets frustrated with school work.

1. *State the problem.*

   Teacher: Those words are offensive to me and to others in the classroom. I've reminded you several times not to use them and it doesn't seem to help. We can't allow them in the classroom. I notice that when things don't go right with your work, you use cuss words to express your anger. How can you help yourself not use those words in school when you're frustrated?

   Andy: But I don't think anything's wrong with them. That's how I feel. Besides, my dad uses those same words when he's driving.

   Teacher: You must decide for yourself what you do out of school but in school, it's against the rules. Besides, it's offensive to me and others. The next time you feel frustrated, what could you do that would not offend other people?

Whether or not the child sees it as a problem for himself, we can let him or her know firmly that it is a problem for others. Living in a community means making compromises for the good of the whole.

2. *Brainstorm solutions.*

   Andy: You could ignore me and pretend you don't hear it.

   Teacher: What else?

   Andy: I could say a different word instead.

   Andy: You could wash my mouth out with soap; that's what my friend's mom does.

   Andy: I could whisper it to myself.

   Teacher: You could miss recess every time you say a cuss word.

3. *Evaluate solutions.*

   • Ignore.

   Teacher: I can't live with that. The words are offensive and I can't ignore them.

   • Different word.

   Andy: Maybe that would work if I found a word that really made me feel good getting it out.

   • Wash with soap.

   Teacher: I won't do that to you. That's not healthy.

   • Whisper.

   Andy: That might work, but I might forget and say it out loud. I'm not sure I can remember to keep it down.

   • Miss recess.

   Teacher: I don't want you to miss recess. It's important for you to get exercise and associate with other kids.

   Andy: I sure don't want to miss it.

4. *Select a solution.* Andy decided to try out a different word. He and his teacher tossed around several suggestions and he finally chose to say "phooey" when he was tempted to say the cuss word.

5. *Try out the solution.* Andy was "phooeying" all over the place.

6. *Decide.* Andy had just about quit using the cuss words, so he and his teacher decided that the problem was almost solved. If he had still been swearing frequently, then they would have had to go back to either Step 2 or 3 and settle on another solution. Perhaps the next time they would try the whispering technique.

Contract for Prevention

After students master the art of thinking this way, we can let them problem solve on their own. Vygotsky (1962/1986) reminds us that the more proficient a child becomes with the process of problem solving, the less scaffolding that child needs. Eventually, students can learn how to fill out a "contract for prevention" independently. A sample contract is shown in Box 8.1.

Students can learn to fill out these contracts on their own. At a convenient time, we can review the contract with them. After a week or so, we can check back to see if the plan is working. If it is, great—they can keep up the good work. If it isn't, then they have to go back to the drawing board and devise a new plan. The second time around, they may need some adult guidance. When students succeed in solving a problem, allowing them to rip up the contract can be a great relief. They messed up, they fixed it, and now they are entitled to proceed with a clean slate.

Problem Solving for Resolving Conflict

The very same problem-solving steps can be used to help students resolve conflicts among themselves. Before they get to the problem-solving stage, however, fighting students must first collect themselves because people can't reason when they are overwhelmed by emotions. Although, at times, conflicts can be settled by moving right into the problem-solving steps, at other times, students may have to be separated and be given time to cool off.

Example Children fighting in the playground over a ball that Fred brought to school.

Box 8.1
Sample Contract for Prevention

This is what happened
   (a preliminary to stating the problem)

This is why I think it happened
   (also a preliminary to stating the problem)

The problem is *(state the problem)*

These are ways I can help it from not happening again
   (brainstorm)

This is what I choose to do so that it won't happen again
   (select a solution)

_____   _____
Signature   Date

---

1. *State the problem.*

   Teacher: So you all want to play with the ball at the same time? I wonder how we can help solve this problem. Let's think of some ideas.

2. *Brainstorm solutions.*

   Fred: I decide. I had it first.

Willy: Let's flip a coin to see who plays with it.

Teacher: I could cut the ball in half.

Gerard: Let's get another ball.

Raoul: Let's play together.

Fred: The teacher can just take the ball and no one will play.

Willy: We'll take turns. Each group will have 5 minutes with the ball.

3. *Evaluate solutions.*
   - Fred keeps it.

     Teacher: The rule is that toys brought to school must be shared. If you don't want to share them, leave them at home.
   - Flip coin.

     Children: That's sort of fair. But then one group never gets the ball.
   - Cut ball in half.

     Children: No way; that would ruin the ball.
   - Another ball.

     Teacher: We don't have another ball to use.
   - Play together.

     Children: We each like different games. That won't work.
   - Teacher takes ball.

     Children: Then no one will get to play. That's not fair.
   - Take turns.

     Children: At least this way we get the ball half the time.

4. *Select a solution.* The students decided to let each group play with the ball for 5 minutes.

They flipped a coin to see which group would go first and the teacher kept track of the time on her watch.

The students and the teacher worked out all the details for implementing this solution so that there wouldn't be additional arguments over the plan.

5. *Try out the solution.* The students played peacefully. In fact, one group asked the other group to join them.
6. *Evaluate the solution.* The fighting stopped.
7. *Decide.* The problem no longer existed. Case closed. At some other time, the teacher could discuss the process with the students and help them see how they could resolve these conflicts on their own in the future.

Often we are tempted to take the fastest route and just decree our solution: "Give me the ball, none of you will have it." But by taking that approach, we lose a "teachable moment." The students learn valuable lessons when resolving conflicts themselves. Nevertheless, before they can resolve their own conflicts, they need us as mediators to guide them in the process. Once they master the approach, they can handle most situations themselves, although there will still be times when students need a mediator for their disputes.

Sometimes, we don't even have to go through all of the problem-solving steps when teaching students how to resolve their conflicts. Many problems are the direct result of miscommunication. By opening up the lines of communication during the first step (stating the problem), the issue gets resolved.

I never saw any of my student teachers so happy to see me as on the day I dropped in on one who was trembling between two warring groups of third-grade girls. The teacher was on the playground with the rest of the class, and the student teacher found herself smack in the middle of a friendship war. Three girls ganged up on one side of her and three on another. The student teacher looked at me with pleading eyes that seemed to say, "Help, rescue me."

"I see you're all very upset. Let's see if we can figure out what the problem is." I pointed to the ringleader of one group and said, "First you tell us what happened. We'll all listen without interrupting." Then I turned to the other leader and said, "After she finishes telling us what happened, you can tell us your version without interruptions."

Leader 1: A few weeks ago, Steven took my half dollar and wouldn't give it back. So today, I took his quarter. The teacher told me to give it back, but I didn't want to because he took my money. Then *she* (pointing to the other leader) told me to give it back.

Me: How did you feel about that? (An important question to teach empathy during the problem-stating step)

Leader 1: Mad. He took my money. Why is she siding with him?

Me (to Leader 2): Now you tell us what happened.

Leader 2: That's right. Steven did take her 50-cent piece. I told her to give the quarter back. I was afraid she'd get in trouble.

Me: So you were scared for her?

Leader 2: Yes.

Me: Oh, so you (Leader 1) were hurt that your friend told you to give the money back, and you (Leader 2) were afraid that your friend was going to get in trouble with the teacher, so that's why you told her to give the money back.

Then a miracle happened. The girls both nodded, smiled, and skipped out to the playground together with their entourage following suit!

So many conflicts arise out of miscommunication. That's why if we teach students listening skills to learn facts and feelings as discussed in Chapter 4, and then encourage them to use these skills right from the start as they begin to problem solve, we can prevent many problems and nip others in the bud (see Resources A and B for conflict resolution resources and programs).

Group Problem Solving

Class meetings provide an ideal opportunity for engaging in group problem solving. If there is a problem that concerns the class as a whole rather than individuals or groups of children, the whole class can engage in group problem solving.

The basic problem-solving steps can provide the structure for class meeting discussions whether students are discussing (a) a problem that has arisen in the class, such as students who have been bickering, the class making too much noise going down the hall, or people not sharing; (b) plans for a field trip; or (c) ideas for future projects. These steps enhance the flow of the discussion and keep the class focused (see Chapter 4).

Example The teacher has received many complaints about the noise level of her students in the hall when they are going to lunch, recess, or special activities.

The teacher calls the class together, sitting in a circle or U-shape if possible.

1. *State the problem.* "Remember how annoying it was for us when we had that incredibly interesting speaker and another class came by so noisily that we could barely hear what she had to say? Well, I have had several complaints from other teachers that our class is disturbing them when we walk through the halls. I wonder what we could do to ensure that we don't disturb anyone else in the school?"

2. *Brainstorm solutions.*

   Lisa: We could tell them to shut their doors.

   Claire: We could keep our hands on our lips to remind us.

   Andy: Anyone who makes noise will miss 10 minutes of recess.

   Hank: We could learn sign language and only use that.

   Al: We could pretend we're on a secret mission.

   Alice: Why can't we just remember to be quiet?

3. *Evaluate solutions.*

   - Shut doors.

     Teacher: I will ask them to shut their doors when possible. But we still need to figure out how to keep it down. They can hear the noise through the doors. Besides, some people are more comfortable with open doors.

   - Hands on lips.

     Jon: I could do that.

Other children agree.

   - Miss recess.

     Students: No, that's not fair.

- Sign language.

  Students: That might be fun.

  Sue: I always wanted to learn sign language.

  Teacher: We could try that, but we need another plan also until we learn enough signing. What could we do now?

- Secret mission.

  Larry: That sounds silly.

  Students: Yes, we're too old for that.

- Just remember.

  Andy: I forget. I need some sort of reminder.

  Al: I get carried away.

4. *Choose a solution.* The students and the teacher voted on the options. They decided to use sign language in the halls but also to keep their fingers to their lips when they are not signing.

5. *Try out the solution.* The students began learning sign language. They kept their fingers to their lips in the halls when they weren't signing.

6. *Evaluate solution.* The noise level of the class in the hall was cut down considerably. The students were enjoying their signing.

7. *Decide.* The problem was solved. If the noise did not stop, then the teacher and the students would meet again and return to either Step 2 for further brainstorming or Step 3 for selecting a different solution.

(For the sake of brevity, only a few suggestions are described here. When we are actually problem solving with a group, many more students will offer their suggestions and will be eager to participate. This process enhances group cohesiveness.)

By engaging our students in the problem-solving process, we are sending a loud and clear message that we have confidence in them and in their ability to take charge of their lives. And in so doing, we provide them with a tool that fosters hope. No matter what has gone wrong in the past, the future can take a different direction.

Summary of Main Points

❖ Problem solving has social as well as academic benefits for students. We must model, teach, and guide our students in the problem-solving process.

❖ Students themselves can use problem solving to figure out how to replace inappropriate behavior with appropriate behavior and how to plan ahead.

❖ The problem-solving steps can provide a structure for resolving conflicts.

❖ Whole classes can engage in group problem solving to resolve whole class issues.

9

Strategies for Chronic, Annoying Misbehaviors

Just as despair can come to one only from other human beings, hope, too, can be given to one only by other human beings.

—Elie Wiesel

Even after we have done all we can to create a classroom atmosphere that is conducive to students behaving appropriately, we may still be faced with chronic misbehaviors, such as tattling, clowning, lying, stealing, cheating, and not completing homework. How can we prevent these problems from sapping our energy? We can look at each chronic misbehaver individually, in terms of the context of that child's life, and try to figure out the source of the problem. Checking cumulative records, talking with the child's previous teachers, carefully listening to and observing the student, and meeting with parents can help us gain insight. What is going on that motivates this child to act inappropriately? Once we become aware of the motivation, we can usually come up with solutions. Nevertheless, sometimes it may not be possible to find out what is causing the misbehavior. Even in those cases, we can still use strategies and techniques suggested in this chapter for dealing with the disruptive behavior.

When dealing with chronic misbehavior, it is important to rule out any physical cause. Vision and hearing deficiencies can cause students to act up. Just imagine a student's frustration trying to learn when he or she can't see or hear properly. A thorough physical exam is advisable when behavior problems become chronic. If we have a student with a behavior problem that seems to persist beyond the norm, we can suggest to the child's parents that the child have a thorough physical exam. If we are uncomfortable suggesting this to the parents, then we can call on the school counselor, psychologist, or social worker to work with the parents and arrange this exam. We can also encourage parents to get their child's teeth checked as well. A kindergarten teacher tried every technique she knew to get one of her students to stop biting his classmates—explaining, isolating, sending him to the principal, even sending him home. Then, one day, the nurse came in to do routine dental exams (unfortunately, a service that many of our schools no longer provide). That child's mouth was riddled with cavities. Once a dentist fixed his teeth, the biting stopped immediately. Wouldn't it be great if all our problems could be solved so easily! Not all problems can be, but some can if we eliminate the physical cause.

Once the physical is ruled out, we can suggest to parents that they also investigate the possibility of neurological problems. The person who completed the physical exam on the child could then refer the child to a neurological exam. Here again, the school counselor, psychologist, or social worker can work with the parents to ensure that neurological problems are ruled out. Physicians and psychologists working together can determine whether a child has a neurologically based learning disability or disease, such as obsessive-compulsive disorder, Tourette's syndrome, or Asperger syndrome. Some children with learning disorders put on disguises so that no one will find out that they feel stupid. They may become the class clowns or act tough and get into fights (Levine, 1994). Some children with Tourette's syndrome or obsessive-compulsive disorder are unable to control some of their inappropriate responses, such as blurting out and engaging in repetitive actions. That's where professionals who understand these disorders can guide us. They can also help these students to understand their disorder and help them develop positive coping mechanisms. Once we have ruled out the physiological and neurological, the next step is to look at what else could be motivating the child's behavior. Then we can discuss solutions for improving the behavior.

Kinds of Misbehaviors

Tattling

Tattling is an incredibly annoying habit: "Teacher, Tim said a bad word." "Teacher, Karen took my ball." "Teacher, Nan took my place in line." When we are bombarded like this, it can really get on our nerves!

Not all tattling is bad. Sometimes tattling can protect another student's safety. Don't we need to be informed when a student's behavior is inappropriate and that student may cause harm to others or to himself or herself? "Teacher, Jake is chasing Nick with a bat." Tattling in situations like this can be helpful.

Sometimes students tell on someone else to determine whether it's okay for them to be doing the same thing. Younger children, particularly kindergartners, may tattle during the years when they are developing a conscience: "Zack's painting at the easel now" may be a child's way of asking, "Is it okay for me to paint at the easel now?"

At other times, negative motives lie beneath children's tattling. Some tell on others to show how much better they are than the one they're tattling on: "Greg's writing on the board when he's not supposed to." Responding with, "That bothers you?" helps us to get at the feelings that caused the tattling and the reasons behind it. In addition, the response, "That bothers you?" seems to take the wind out of some children's sails. The fact that we don't overreact, and instead throw the ball back to the tattler, removes his or her need for tattling. By engaging in reflective listening, reflecting back to the student that he or she is bothered by the other child's behavior, we can identify the true source of the feelings. The child's response might help us figure out why he or she feels the need to tattle. We may find that the student is diverting our attention away from something inappropriate that he or she did. Perhaps the student feels that Greg is favored or gets more attention. Perhaps the student feels left out and excluded.

Sometimes students tell on their classmates just to get them in trouble. Rather than trying to make themselves look good, they're trying to make someone else look bad. This might be a student who has poor self-esteem as a result of failure at school tasks or perhaps because that student has been unduly criticized by others. Listening, observing, and thinking about the situation helps us gain insight into the problem. To help stop this kind of tattling, we can try to provide the tattler with ego-building experiences, such as being asked to run errands or to take on responsibilities.

Have you noticed that students are much more likely to tattle if we intervene in their fights when they come running to us to tell on a classmate? Keeping ourselves out of the battle by not taking sides and helping our students use the problem-solving process to resolve their own disputes can eliminate this source of tattling.

Clowning

Class clowns are so disruptive to our teaching that it is no wonder we sometimes think they're deliberately out to get us. Some may be, but most are just trying to cover up their own inadequacies and worries. Some students may use clowning to cover a deficiency, becoming Jerry Seinfeld or Eddie Murphy during math time as a foil for their inability to do math problems. These students may be using clowning to distract us from noticing their weakness. Making them aware of their pattern of behavior by saying, "I notice that when we are doing difficult work in math, you clown around. Perhaps you don't really understand the material?" can help eliminate this problem.

For other students, clowning becomes their vehicle for achieving success. Students who feel unpopular, unnoticed, or disliked may resort to clowning to gain acceptance and recognition from their peers. They get recognition and fame for their comedic abilities, which they could not otherwise get. Steering them to more positive sources of recognition and acceptance can ameliorate the problem. But if they're really humorous, why not cut a deal with them: "If you can keep your jokes to yourself during the day, during the last 10 minutes of the school day, you can have the stage to tell jokes."

Other students may be overburdened and highly stressed. They may have tremendous pressures in their lives. For example, some may be overprogrammed and have no time to breathe between extra-curricular activities, some may feel pressure from having a high-achieving older sibling, some may worry about meeting their parents' expectations for high grades, and some may be experiencing home problems, such as a family member's sickness or a divorce. Some of these students clown to relieve their tension. Working together with their parents to figure out how to reduce some of the stress would be beneficial. Also, learning stress reduction techniques may be helpful to these students. Some others may clown because they have short attention spans. Breaking their work into smaller segments and then gradually increasing the length of the segments can help them.

Figuring out the source of a student's clowning can help us determine what to do about it. Keeping records of the who, what, when, where, and how (see Chapter 6) can help us pinpoint which of the above reasons is the source of the clowning. Then, once we have figured out the source of the problem, privately discussing with the student the pattern of the clowning behavior and why it's disruptive to the class and counterproductive for him or her, and then helping the student figure out strategies for meeting his or her needs without being disruptive, can be beneficial.

Lying

Lying has different meanings for different ages. Many pre-schoolers do not know the difference between reality and fantasy. What may seem to us to be a lie may just be normal imaginative thinking for children their age. Nevertheless, kindergarten children and older students should be able to understand the difference between reality and fantasy. Their exaggerations and untruths are usually intentionally concocted to deceive. Untruths that are usually designed as a solution to a child's problem are the focus of our discussion on lying.

Possible sources. Sometimes children tell lies to protect their self-images. Children often feel that lies can help them mask their vulnerable points and inflate their image in front of others. Children may choose to tell a lie when they feel *ashamed* of what they have or have not done. For example, Frank told his mom that they didn't have any math tests that week. He was ashamed to admit he had failed the math test.

Children may choose to tell a lie when they feel *afraid*. When I was in kindergarten, I told the teacher I was allergic to butter because

I was afraid she would force me to eat the butter we had just churned, and I hated the taste and smell of butter. All the other children were excited to taste it.

Children may choose to tell a lie when they *feel insecure and fear rejection*. For example, Tommy lied when he said he hated playing ball because he was worried that he would be the last one picked to be on a team. Children may choose to tell a lie to *cover a deficiency*. For example, Michelle was very forgetful. She forgot to do her homework. She told her teacher that a bully tore it up on the bus on the way to school. Michelle told a lie so that she would not be labeled "forgetful" or "spacey" again, as she had been in the past.

Sometimes children tell lies to *protect themselves from punishment*. For example, Tom denied hitting Joe on the playground because he was afraid the teacher would call his mother and then she would ground him. Sometimes children tell lies *if they think we're too strict with them*. They feel they have to sneak to do what students their age are normally allowed to do.

What we can do when students lie. The best response is to express concern about their need to lie: "I wonder why you couldn't tell me what really happened?" Because we show concern calmly, this approach makes it easier for students to talk about the reason they felt compelled to lie. Stay calm and encourage them to discuss why they felt they needed to tell a lie: "I lied because I was afraid you'd call my mother and she would ground me for a week."

Separate our own issues and feelings from the discussion. Try not to overreact. If we overreact and get furious at students, they'll learn not to trust us and perhaps be tempted to tell even bigger lies in the future. Focus on the child's feelings that led him or her to lie rather than on our own feelings of betrayal that the student's lie aroused.

Sometimes lies are blown out of proportion by adults. Labeling a student a liar or overreacting and treating that student as if he or she will end up in the penitentiary if the lying keeps up will likely cause the student to feel hopeless about being truthful. Many adults say to children, "If you tell me the truth, I won't punish you." This is not always an honest, realistic promise because the misbehavior may be so serious that it would require a consequence. Instead, it might be more appropriate to say, "If you tell me what really happened, we can figure out what to do about this situation and perhaps I can help you not to let this happen again." The student will be more willing to be cooperative if he or she is not afraid of our wrath and revenge, even if we do have to enforce a consequence.

When we are positive that a child is not telling the truth, we should confront the child and not beat around the bush. Say, "I understand that you did bend that spoon in the cafeteria" rather than ask, "Did you bend that spoon in the cafeteria?" if we know full well that the student bent the spoon. If a student is standing in front of a broken window with a baseball bat in his hand and a baseball on the other side of the window, what is the point of asking, "Who broke the window?" We know, the student knows, and a question like that will only put the student on the defensive and make it tempting for him to lie and not admit that he did it.

Encourage students to be honest about their feelings. When children are pressured to cover up their true emotions, it's confusing for them. We often squelch children's feelings from a very young age. Expressions such as "Don't cry," "Be brave even if it hurts," "Calm down, don't get too excited," "Say you're sorry even if you're not," and "Don't be angry" confuse children. This confusion sometimes leads to lying to cover up how they really feel. They say they feel a certain way because they think that's what the adult wants to hear. See Chapter 4 for further discussion on how we can help our students express their feelings openly and honestly.

Use the problem-solving approach to help the child tackle the problem that caused him or her to tell a lie in the first place. Ask the student, "How could you have avoided the problem in the first place so that you wouldn't feel that you had to lie?" or "How could you have told the truth and not suffered negative consequences?" The student could work with us to come up with some alternative suggestions. Frank, who was ashamed to admit to his mother that he failed the math test, could have told his mom he didn't understand math and asked her to get him extra help. I could have told the teacher that I never eat butter. Michelle could have tried to figure out a signal to remind herself not to forget her work. Tommy could practice playing ball at home to improve his skills. Problem solving helps our students learn that there are many alternatives to not telling the truth.

If a student seems to lie frequently, it helps to try to find a pattern to the lies. Do they revolve around homework? A certain subject? Friends? By detecting a pattern—frequency, duration, topic—we may be able to gain insight into the behavior. It always helps to make students conscious of this pattern. Sometimes, the behavior may stop quickly if it is brought to their attention. If the problem persists, then it would be advisable to check with the parents to see if this is a problem at home as well and to work with the parents to help the child. On occasion, referring the child to professional help may be warranted.

Stealing

Young children have a difficult time differentiating between what belongs to them and what belongs to others. For example, a kinder-gartner who loved school took things home with him from the classroom. He did not intend to steal but, rather, just wanted to keep a reminder of school with him. But older children, first grade and up, should know the difference between what's theirs and what's some-one else's.

Possible reasons for stealing. Sometimes students steal to get back at someone at whom they are angry. They may take something from that person just to hurt them. A student who is annoyed at the teacher for setting down an unacceptable limit may steal a trinket off the teacher's desk. If a child is annoyed at a classmate, he or she may steal a pencil from that classmate.

Some students steal out of impulsiveness—they want something when they want it and they'll take it from someone else if they have to. Rich or poor, it does not matter. For example, Mike loved the soccer ball eraser on top of Sean's pencil. He thought it would be a great addition to his collection of erasers, so he took it.

Some students steal because they feel they need something so desperately, they just can't do without it. They see no way of getting what they need other than stealing. For example, Gwen stole two dollars from the teacher's desk because she had forgotten her money for the field trip and was afraid if she didn't hand it in that day, she wouldn't be able to go. Some deprived children steal because they don't have what they need. They may take others' food because they are hungry or someone else's pen because they don't have one.

What we can do about stealing. First of all, we need to keep our cool. Labeling the child a thief can deeply wound the child and can hurt our relationship with the child. The student made a mistake and it's up to us to help that child learn not to repeat the same mistake. To do so, we have to keep the lines of communication open so that they will feel free to tell us what's on their minds, without worrying about our being judgmental.

If we are certain that a child has stolen something, then directly letting him or her know that we know helps deter the child from lying about it: "That's Sean's eraser. Please return it to him." "I saw you take the money from the drawer; please put it back. It doesn't belong to you."

When we don't know for sure, then it's best to help the child feel comfortable admitting that he or she took something: "Sometimes it's tempting to take things from others." "I could see why you might have done that." "Could you please help us find the eraser?" "The bell is missing from my desk. Would whoever borrowed it please return it?"

If we can't prove that a child stole something even if we strongly suspect that he or she did, we have to let it go, because we might be accusing the wrong child. In our American justice system, people are innocent until proven guilty. Someone stole 50 dollars from a teacher's purse in October. She strongly suspected Tony but could never prove her case. Months later, on field day, the teacher gave each child a quarter to buy a popsicle. When she came to Tony, she said "You have plenty of money. I don't need to give you any more today." She gave every student except Tony a quarter. Yes, this is indeed a true story! The teacher harbored her resentment to this child all year long and assumed the child was guilty of stealing her money even though she couldn't prove it. What an injustice to this possibly innocent child! If we can't prove something, we have to let it go.

Once we have ascertained that a student has indeed stolen something, of course we should require the student to return the merchandise. If the student no longer has the object, then having him or her replace it or make monetary restitution is the fair thing to do. But most important, engage the student in a discussion that helps him or her process the ramifications of stealing; for example, it may seem like a good idea at the moment, but it has much more of a down side than an up side, including the stress on the student's conscience. Help the student figure out his or her options other than stealing, to help prevent a recurrence of the situation: "What could I have done to get enough money for the field trip other than stealing it?" Most children do experience pangs of conscience, worry when they steal, and will be responsive to such a conversation. Severely disturbed children, however, may be numb and may not feel remorse. In such situations, referring them to the school counselor and further professional help is advisable, in addition to conducting this conversation with them.

If the stealing pattern continues and does not seem to be related to a specific event or situation, then contacting the home and trying to work together with the parents would be important. Referring the child to professional help might also be advisable.

Cheating

As with stealing, very young children do not understand the concept of cheating. They are encouraged to learn from each other and to copy each other: "Try to build a tower with the blocks just like Billy did." "Look at Sue's picture to figure out what to do." But once children enter the first grade, they learn the difference between copying to learn from someone and copying to cover up that they don't know something. Very quickly, they learn the meaning of a test and all of its implications.

Possible reasons for cheating. Students may cheat if our expectations for them are too high. They may not be capable of mastering the material, yet they are expected to. The only way out that they can see is to cheat to get good marks to bring home.

Some students may cheat simply because they are not prepared. Perhaps something else going on in their lives took priority, or perhaps they were just not in the mood to study. They might write answers on their hands or ask to go to the bathroom to check the notebook with answers that they have hidden in their pocket.

Test anxiety can also be the source of some cheating. A student may have studied hard but may be too anxious to think. The only way out that the student can see is to cheat. Some students cheat because they have become used to taking the easy way out in life. They have not been held accountable for their actions and have not been required to assume responsibilities. Why study when they can get the answers from the person next to them? Why bother reading the book when someone else can summarize it for them?

What we can do when students cheat. As with lying and stealing, if we are sure that a student cheated, why play games and why ask them? We can simply let them know that we know what they did. This should be done in private. Humiliating a student in front of his or her peers will only antagonize the student, hurt our rapport with him or her, and will get in the way of our being able to have an open and honest discussion with that student about the problem. By listening to the student, we can likely determine the source of the cheating.

Of course, if our expectations are too high, then we can readjust them. If something else is going on in the student's life, we can take this into consideration. We may also be able to help the student figure out how to juggle his or her various responsibilities. If test anxiety is the issue, some relaxation techniques might help. Speaking to a school counselor might also be helpful.

If we are sure that the student is cheating just to take the easy way out, then administering that student's test individually may make sense if it is feasible. Also, not giving credit for the work that we know was copied from others would be in order. But we should try to be as sure as we can that this is the reason. Rather than our jumping to this conclusion right away, it's helpful to eliminate other causes of cheating first. Don't we all deserve the benefit of the doubt?

Not Completing Homework

Getting some children to complete their homework can be a constant drain on us. Let's look at some possible reasons why students may not consistently do their homework and what we can do about it.

What about the homework itself? Is it too hard? Too boring? Does the student see no point to it? Does it seem unnecessarily long? Could the material be mastered with a shorter assignment? Adjusting our homework assignments so that they are meaningful, reasonable in length, and "do-able" independently by the student may be all that it takes. Explaining the purpose of each assignment to our students helps us clarify for ourselves whether it is really necessary and makes it more likely that students will do the work. Dividing assignments into smaller segments may make them more manageable for some children. Of course, working cooperatively with other teachers so that students are not overburdened with assignments on one particular night is helpful.

What is our attitude to homework? It's very important to check homework daily. If we don't bother to check the homework, then our students may assume that it's not important. Reviewing the homework assignment with the class and at least cursorily checking students' work shows them that we consider this work to be important and that we want to be sure that they understand what they are learning.

Being aware of the child's home environment is critical. Some children may not have either time or space set aside for them to do their work at home. We can try to enlist parental support, encouraging parents to have a set homework time for their children and to keep the television off during this time. After-school programs can provide assistance for students who might otherwise receive none at home.

Some students may simply be forgetful, especially if homework is not assigned every evening. We can help forgetful students figure out a reminder for themselves, such as a note attached to their bookbag or even a string around their finger. Many schools give every student an assignment notebook or require them to purchase one on their own. That way there's a set place for assignments to be recorded. Reviewing the homework assignments at the end of the day can also be beneficial. Some teachers find it helpful to have a telephone tree where students call each other for homework reminders and help.

Some children have never had responsibilities and, consequently, do not know how to handle them. Gradually introducing students to responsibility by dividing assignments into shorter segments and helping them figure out reminders for themselves can help get them used to assuming responsibilities in a nonthreatening fashion. Sending letters encouraging parents to give their children some responsibilities at home could also help solve this problem.

Summary of Main Points

❖ Physiological and neurological problems can trigger misbehavior.

❖ Understanding misbehavior in the context of a child's life can lead to solutions for eliminating misbehavior.

❖ Many sources can exist for the same behavior problem. Solutions must be tailored to the source of the child's problem.

10

Strategies for Misbehavior Resulting From Childhood Trauma

This we know: All things are connected like the blood that unites us, we did not weave the web of life, we are merely a strand in it. Whatever we do to the web, we do to ourselves.
—Chief Seattle

Some students carry more than their bookbags to school each day. They haul the invisible baggage of trauma straight into our classrooms. And what do they unpack? Pain, masquerading in the guise of misbehavior and underachievement. Unable or unwilling to verbalize their horrors, these children express them in actions instead, actions that are often discipline nightmares for teachers.

What are we teachers to do? We feel sorry for these students, but we can't ignore their disruptive behavior just because they have gone through hard times. It's not helpful to them and, besides, we have a whole room full of students to consider. We cannot allow students with problems to be so disruptive that they deny their classmates the right to their education. Nor can we be therapists. We have more than enough on our plates already. Yet, these students are also entitled to an education. Our classrooms may be their only hope for a better future and their only respite from pain and discouragement. School may be their haven.

Fortunately, there are steps we can take that will help these students, steps that can make life more pleasant for everyone in the classroom and provide quality educational experiences for all of our students. The key lies in understanding the origins of students' dysfunctional behavior that stem from trauma so that we can use effective teaching strategies to administer antidotes to the poisons in their systems.

In most cases, there is little that we can do to change these students' lives beyond the schoolhouse doors. But within our doors, there is much we can do to create an atmosphere of acceptance and caring. What we *can* do is help them become more resilient so that they can withstand the pathogenic pressures in their lives and recover and bounce back to normal functioning (Redl, 1969). We can help them learn skills that will foster their resilience, that will help them work toward becoming successful survivors and positive participants in the classroom community.

What Is Childhood Trauma?

First, let's look at what constitutes childhood trauma. Childhood trauma is "the mental result of one sudden external blow or a series of blows, rendering the young person temporarily helpless and breaking past ordinary coping and defensive operations" (Terr, 1991, p. 11). Experiences that go beyond normal life stresses—such as physical, sexual, or emotional abuse; neglect; divorce; parental alcoholism; parental illness or handicap; death in the family; foster care; and physical injury—can be traumatic for children. Ordinary life stresses, such as having a new sibling, moving, or going to school for the first time, do not fall into the definition of childhood trauma. They may be stressful for the child, but these are transitory, and, under ordinary circumstances, children can adjust to them and cope with daily living. As such, the stresses are not considered to be traumatic but, rather, are just stepping stones in children's development.

Unfortunately, childhood trauma seems to be more common than we might suspect. When studying the effects of trauma on children, psychiatrist Lenore Terr discovered that many children in her control groups—that is, those whom she and her team of researchers had selected because they ostensibly had not undergone a trauma—had also suffered severe scares or full-blown traumas, leading her to conclude that there is apparently a lot of unrecognized, but real, psychic trauma in the world of normal children (Terr, 1990). For some children, we may know the nature of their horror, but for others, it remains hidden. Trauma is the source of many serious, persistent discipline problems, whether we know of the trauma or not. That's why understanding the nature of trauma can provide insight into the behavior of some children and into discipline approaches that will be successful for them.

Much of children's behavior is profoundly affected by their trauma: "An ever-draining, ever-present abscess forms. The child goes on living an ordinary life. But if something touches the traumatic abscess, the child hurts" (Terr, 1990, p. 191). A Vietnamese child who had witnessed horrors in his native country was being tested for grade placement in his new American school. Everything was going well between him and his tester until she brought out a puzzle of a person, dumped it on the table, and asked the child to put the puzzle together. The child ran out of the room screaming. In his native country, he had witnessed mutilations; the puzzle pieces triggered his memory of that horror. We may not always be able to detect trauma, but the effects may surface at any time.

Often, however, children send us signals that they are hurting. Misbehavior and underachievement are red flags frantically waved by many traumatized students. For a variety of reasons, both developmental and situational, most traumatized children cannot verbalize "Help, I'm in pain," and instead they express these feelings in actions. They may lash out at others, deliberately annoy us, become passive, cling and whine, get jumpy, or produce very poor work. By understanding trauma, we can see many of our students in a new light, similar to the perceptual psychology picture of the vase and the faces—whether you see a vase or a face depends on how you look at it. Not every student with severe behavior problems has been traumatized, but a significant number of them have. That's why it is helpful to understand the nature of trauma. By looking at a student's behavior in the context of his or her life, we can gain insight into determining appropriate discipline strategies. Cumulative records as well as school counselors, psychologists, and social workers are sources for us to check to ascertain whether a particular student has had a traumatic life experience. Parents also often confide that information to us. In some cases, we may not be able to find out such information because it may be a tightly guarded secret. Nevertheless, even if the child has not experienced a trauma, or if we have no way of determining whether the student has experienced a trauma even though we may suspect it, the strategies in this chapter can be helpful.

The behavior and learning problems discussed in this chapter are commonly found among traumatized children. Despite this fact, this chapter is not meant to be used for the purpose of diagnosing trauma. These behaviors are not in and of themselves indicators of trauma. For example, just because a child is aggressive does not mean the child has been abused or otherwise traumatized. Just because a child cannot read does not mean that images of trauma are blocking his or her mind; the child may have a neurological impairment such as attention deficit disorder (ADD). In those cases when we already know or strongly suspect that a student has suffered a trauma, the information in this chapter can help us to understand the problem in the context of the child's life and to design appropriate solutions to the problem.

Our Role

Can we teachers make a difference when we interact with a child for just a few hours a day, for less than a year? Can we teachers really help without devoting our full attention to one child or becoming therapists? Absolutely! Study after study confirms that teachers can have a profound impact on the lives of traumatized children. As discussed in the introduction, long-term studies have confirmed that most children with problems who grow into well-adjusted adults have had at least one significant adult during their childhood who validated them, cared about them, and made them feel worthwhile. No, we can't save them all, as much as we would like to, but we can save many. How? First, mainly by noticing them and taking an interest in them, expressing our belief in them, encouraging them, and treating them with empathy and respect (Werner & Smith, 1992; Zimrin, 1986), being what Alice Miller (1990) calls an "enlightened witness." At times, this may be easier said than done because these students' behaviors can be so offensive and frustrating. But the nice part is that it doesn't take much time. Just a reassuring look or an encouraging comment, or even a smile given periodically throughout the day, can be a tremendous boost to a child's self-confidence. "She likes me" can help motivate the child to cooperate. Second, we can create a secure environment in which they can flourish—one with structure, limits, and predictability. Third, we can teach them skills of resilience: how to manage their anger, express themselves constructively, and solve their own problems.

Behavior Problems That Could Be Manifestations of Trauma

Now let's look at some of the more common and more disruptive behavior problems that can be manifestations of childhood trauma and what can be done about them. Keep in mind that, although what we do in the classroom is certainly helpful and necessary for the extreme cases, such as those discussed in this chapter, these students also need more individual guidance in handling their problems than we can possibly provide them in the classroom. That's where school counselors and other psychological professionals come into play. By working with them and soliciting their suggestions, we don't have to face this task alone, and we can collaborate to work in the best interest of our students.

Hurting Others Without Seeming to Care

Some children hurt others and do not even seem to care that they have inflicted pain. Frank whacks Tom and then proceeds to laugh at Tom for being such a crybaby. Marie scratches a deep gouge into Ann's arm. She leaves Ann crying and goes off to play with another group of girls. We ask ourselves, "How can these children be so cold and cruel?" " What kind of monsters are they?"

Origin

Excruciating Pain and Suffering. Far from being monsters, these children probably have undergone excruciating pain themselves, either physical or psychological, or both. Having been hurt so often, they finally close off their minds from feeling. As a way to tolerate their suffering, they completely repress their feelings (Polansky, Chalmers, Buttenwieser, & Williams, 1981). Doesn't it make sense that they would numb themselves to block out their pain? But no longer feeling pain, they lack a concept of pain. They don't know what hurt is, either for themselves or for others; *hurt* has become a foreign word. "The repression of our suffering destroys our empathy for the suffering of others" (Miller, 1990, p. 13). As a result, these children totally lack empathy—a very dangerous situation. Some may feel "Because I was hurt, I'll hurt others. Nobody cares about me, so why should I care about anyone else?"

Discipline Strategies

Direct Confrontation. Even if they are ignorant about pain, no children should ever be allowed to hurt others, either physically or verbally: "Stop that. When you poke Billy with the ruler it hurts." "Please don't use those words. They are hurtful."

Acknowledge Their Hurts. "That must have hurt when you fell off the swing." "Boy, that scratch sure looks like it stings." These students must recognize their own pain to be sensitive to the pain of others. By putting their feelings into words, we help them accomplish this. At first, they may deny that they are feeling pain and act as if they do not know what we are talking about. "It's no big deal. I can't even feel it." That's okay. We still need to remind them when they are hurt so that we can reawaken their feelings. It makes sense that, at first, numbed children would deny their feelings. We can help them see that pain is like a fire alarm that warns people to cry for help (Terr, 1990). Once they learn to hear that fire alarm, they may have a very exaggerated response to their pain. "Ooeeoooowwww!" they scream. Don't worry, this is a common reaction when senses are reawakened. They'll settle down to normal response levels shortly.

Cultivate Empathic Skills. Chapter 4 describes how we can develop empathy in our students. The nice part of developing this skill is that all our students benefit from this training. The difference between teaching empathic skills to our whole class and to students who hurt others without seeming to care because they have been numbed by trauma is one of degree, not of kind.

Aggressiveness

Some children seem to be constantly fighting with others. They pick fights for trivial reasons. They are aggressive and rarely hesitate to hit when angry.

Origin

Abuse is highly correlated with excessive aggression in children (Lewis, Shanok, Pincus, & Glaser, 1980; Reidy, 1977). Why do abused children lash out aggressively?

Modeling. Children identify with their parents. Abused children are no exception. As part of the process of identification, children copy parental behavior whether or not the behavior is worthy of copying (Bandura, 1973). If parents generally hit their children, then their children will hit others. If parents have no impulse control and lash out when they are angry, their children will learn to do the same, almost as if by osmosis.

Rage. Doesn't it make sense that abused children would be full of rage? Rage silently foments inside abused children because if they let out their anger, it would antagonize their abusers and generate further mistreatment. But rage can boil within only for so long before spilling out somewhere. So, abused children spill their rage on "safe" targets, such as classmates and teachers, rather than on those who instigate it. Displacement is an unconscious mechanism for moving anger onto others (Terr, 1990).

Sometimes, rage takes on the complete opposite appearance to aggression: passivity. Rather than externalizing the rage, some students, especially girls, turn the rage inward to themselves, essentially beating up on themselves. Many see themselves as bad or defective and may hurt themselves or become suicidal (Terr, 1990). This can be an even more dangerous situation than externalized aggression.

Power Over Helplessness. There is absolutely nothing children can do to protect themselves from powerful, abusive adults. Many abused children are terrified of reexperiencing the utter helplessness and powerlessness they suffered during abuse. When they fear that their safety or self-esteem may be threatened again, they try to replace helplessness with power by becoming aggressive and lashing out. Boys, in particular, tend to use aggression to protect themselves against feeling helpless (Briere, 1992). Researchers have found that even toddlers and preschoolers who suffer from hidden family violence exhibit higher than normal aggression. Although these very young children inhibit their aggressiveness with adults they perceive to be more powerful, they lash out at peers and even adults whom they perceive to be less powerful (Fisher & Ayoub, 1993).

Discipline Strategies

Modeling. Modeling is just common sense. We can be an alternative model and hope that our students will identify with us. Does that mean we can't get angry? Certainly not. We're only human. All we need to do is to try not to overreact. We can separate our feelings from impulsive actions so that we can express ourselves constructively and nonhurtfully.

Anger Harnessing. Chapter 5 discusses how we can deal with a raging student and how we can help our students learn how to harness their anger. Helping the very angry child choose a strategy and a cooling-off zone for those times when we or the student notice that he or she is about to lose it can be a lifesaver. Enlisting the support of the school counselor or other school personnel, such as the principal, if your school does not have a counselor, may be necessary for a child with uncontrollable rage.

When passive students emerge from their passivity, they may become extremely aggressive initially. Even though it is difficult for us, externalizing aggression is actually progress because it can be accessed and dealt with more directly than their passivity.

Empowerment. Positive sources of power and control over their own destiny can help alleviate aggression that is a response to powerlessness. Involving the aggressive child in choosing a strategy and a cooling-off zone when he or she is about to lose it gives that student a sense of power and control over his or her actions. Being given opportunities to make decisions, to choose among acceptable options, to have a say in classroom rules (see Chapter 2), and to engage in the problem-solving process (see Chapter 8) can also channel their need for power in positive directions.

Deliberately Annoying Others

Some children seem to be willing to do anything to deliberately annoy us or their classmates. They tap on desks, drop pencils, constantly interrupt, argue over everything, and often go out of their way to disobey.

Origin

Helplessness. Abused children frequently have no idea when they will be hit. One day they may be slapped for not cleaning their plate properly and another for just being in the way. The helplessness of not knowing when they will be punished is overwhelming. That's why some abused children take defensive action. They are deliberately provocative so that they can control the timing of their punishment and can brace themselves as if to say, "I will misbehave so that I can be in control and will know exactly when I will be punished" (Green, 1985).

Rejection. "I know I'm going to be rejected so I'll reject you before you reject me" is the logic of some abused and neglected children. They keep their distance from us, rejecting our overtures, because they are afraid that we will abandon them also. Because of their maltreatment, they do not feel worthy. They protect themselves from further hurt by playing it safe and not allowing us to get close to them.

Starving for Attention. Many neglected children crave attention. Many so desperately want to be touched and noticed that they will even provoke punishment to get attention. For them, no attention is far more painful than harsh attention (Lewis & Balla, 1976).

Discipline Strategies

Predictable Environment. Knowing the routines of the day—when they eat, when they go to recess, when they study math—reassures students that order, not chaos, is the modus operandi in the classroom. Clearly stated rules that let students know in advance what is expected of them and consequences that are fair and meaningful can have a reassuring effect. Does that mean we can't deviate from our schedule? Certainly not. That would be impossible in a school setting. All sorts of interruptions occur—plays, field trips, schoolwide programs. But if our routines are changed, these children need to know well in advance, if possible, to eliminate the element of the unexpected and to build their trust. "What are they going to spring on me next?" many students think. Advanced preparation helps remove the fear of randomness and helplessness that is the source of much provocative behavior.

Attention. Children who annoy are often ignored because "they are just looking for attention." Yes, they are looking for attention. Why? Because they crave it, and, if we don't acknowledge them, they will attempt to get our attention in disruptive ways. They may interrupt, make annoying sounds, or pick fights with others. They will do whatever they have to avoid being ignored. Sincerely praising them for improvement or accomplishments is positive attention. Giving them responsibilities in the classroom, such as taking care of a pet, delivering messages, or erasing the blackboards, is positive attention. Calling when they are absent or listening to their ideas is positive attention. Having them share a hobby or special knowledge will also work. Whatever we can do to engage them so that they have a feeling of belonging and usefulness will give them their sorely needed positive recognition, which will encourage them to seek attention in more socially acceptable ways. Letting them know that we believe in them, that they do matter, and that they are basically good people inside, even if at times they may be incredibly annoying on the outside, can make all the difference in the world for some.

Hypervigilance

Some students always seem to be on the lookout for potential dangers. They are fearful, suspicious, and mistrustful and are so acutely sensitive to mood, tone of voice, facial expression, and bodily movement that they can make the rest of us extremely uncomfortable. So much of their energy is diverted to their "frozen watchfulness" (Ounstead, Oppenheimer, & Lindsay, 1974) that they are inattentive to the lessons we are teaching, their learning is compromised (Green, 1985), and they become a discipline problem for us.

Origin

Unpredictability. Often a traumatic event hits a person unexpectedly, as in the case of an accident, a tornado, or abuse. Victims of trauma often remain constantly on guard long after the traumatic event because they fear a recurrence. If it could happen once, it makes sense that it could happen again. Children especially remain on guard in the outside world lest an event occur that might trigger the same feelings of helplessness, panic, and loss.

Discipline Strategies

Predictability. As we discussed previously, clearly stated routines, rules, and consequences that are consistently followed will gradually help reduce these children's hyperalertness. If we try not to overreact and use our own self-control, gradually they will learn to be more trusting of us and our classrooms.

Jumpiness/Hyperactivity

Some children can never seem to sit still. Their hyperactive behavior can truly get on our nerves because it is so disruptive to classroom functioning.

Origin

Sometimes this problem can be attributed to attention deficit disorder (ADD) and other disorders. But let's be careful about attaching the ADD label to children—some children are just more active, others have food allergies, for example, and others might exhibit hyperactive behavior because of trauma. If we know or suspect that a student has suffered a trauma, we might explore the possibility of the hyperactivity being a manifestation of post-traumatic stress disorder. If this is the case, then we can better deal with the problem if we examine the hyperactive behavior in the context of the child's life experience.

Physioneurosis. Brain chemistry changes after trauma (LeDoux, 1989). Because the threshold for alarm is lowered, trauma victims often react to ordinary moments as if they were emergencies. Abraham Kardiner labeled this reaction "physioneurosis" in connection with soldiers (Kardiner, 1941). Not just people who have been to war but also people who have suffered any kind of trauma often experience physioneurosis. Their autonomic nervous systems appear to continue to prepare them for action. Jumpy and guarded, they are on alert for the emergency that no longer exists ("Post-traumatic stress: Part I," 1991). When something unexpected does occur, even though it may seem trivial and uneventful to us, it may trigger hyperactivity in the trauma victim. For example, if you've ever been sideswiped by another car, you may cringe and jump whenever you see a car coming within a few feet of your car, while someone who has not had that sideswiping experience probably does not react at all to such a situation.

Intrusive Memories. Trauma "creates permanent mental pictures. Vivid ones. Moving pictures" (Terr, 1990, p. 170). In studies of child victims of trauma, Lenore Terr discovered that children often see videotapes of their traumas in their minds. The only way some children can shut off these frightful tapes is to stay active. Hyperactivity distracts them from the visions in their minds. Because of these tapes, they may not be able to concentrate; they may flit from one activity to another; and they may disrupt the classroom (Sandberg, 1987).

Discipline Strategies

Predictability. The more routinized that life is in the classroom, the greater the possibility that these students will be able to lower their guard and calm down.

Open Discussion. When students do overreact to a situation, we can talk them through it—reassuring them that no danger exists and that they are not crazy—they have a good reason (their trauma) for responding this way. By openly discussing physioneurosis (in simple terms) with them, we can eventually help them to understand and control their own responses: "Sometimes, when people have had scary experiences, they become jumpy. They are extra sensitive when something unexpected happens. That's normal. When that does happen, you can tell yourself that 'I'm jumpy because of what happened before, but now is different. Everything will be okay.' " Encouraging them to take a few deep breaths might help them settle down.

Involvement. Perhaps the best solution to this problem is, whenever possible, to keep our students so involved in what they are studying that their minds stay focused on something other than their trauma. If they have a special interest, a passion, so much the better. If they can't sit still, we can give them a task that requires activity. The one thing to guard against is empty time—that's when the frightful videotapes are most likely to turn back on. These students need to stay busy. Often they are the ones who, when we tell everyone to put their heads on their desks and be quiet, do something to disrupt the silence. They have to. It's the only way to shut off the horrifying videotapes.

Spaciness

Some children become trancelike in school. Although this spaciness could be a sign of epilepsy or some other physical disorder, it can also be a sign of post-traumatic stress. Traumatized children may appear "spacey" and forgetful, and these children frequently daydream. Some may read the words on a page but do not process the information. They dissociate themselves from the present, removing their minds to another time and place.

Origin

Overwhelming Thoughts and Feelings. We all dissociate at times. Our minds wander during a lecture, we tune ourselves out in uncomfortable situations. Dissociation is a normal mental process and it is particularly normal and common for children. Children daydream, "forget" instantly, and often hear only what they want to hear. Because children are normative dissociators, traumatized children can readily call on dissociation to help them cope with their traumas. They can easily mentally go off into another place and separate their minds from their bodies so that they are not consciously aware of the overwhelming pain, thoughts, and feelings triggered by their trauma. Their ability to dissociate is, in fact, what saves them from becoming totally overwhelmed by the horrors they face: "Dissociation is adaptive: it allows relatively normal functioning for the duration of the traumatic event and leaves a large part of the personality unaffected by the trauma" (van der Kolk, 1987, pp. 185-186).

Problems arise for us in the classroom because dissociation usually persists beyond the initial traumatic event. Traumatized students often dissociate to defend themselves against any event that might trigger memories of their initial suffering. They may become spacey if a theme generally related to protection, harm, or abandonment appears in their school work. They may become spacey and dissociative in school when they experience an echo of their painful experience. Even a seemingly innocuous story in a reading book could trigger this experience. Or these children may just block off their minds from any new knowledge, out of fear of what Pandora's box it might open (Donovan & McIntyre, 1990).

As we might expect, children who suffer from secret family violence may have great difficulties concentrating on their work and remembering what they should be doing. Their energies are primarily focused on guarding the family secret. Some put on "cognitive blinders" so that they will not be aware that they are aware. Accordingly, they do not allow themselves to know what they know and to tell what they know, which is a great impediment to classroom learning (Donovan & McIntyre, 1990).

Discipline Strategies

All too often these students are labeled as learning disabled because their external symptoms are similar to those of learning-disabled students. A problem is that the direct teaching strategies that are appropriate for truly learning disabled students will often not work for traumatized children. What traumatized students need is help processing their trauma to unblock their minds, not tips on how to process their learning. Individual counseling is certainly critical for these students, but we can also try to help them by refocusing, creating awareness, and helping them identify and sort out their feelings.

Refocusing. Notice when they go off in a trance and try to gently bring them back. Help them to refocus, perhaps by softly calling their name, making eye contact, or gently tapping them on the shoulder.

Creating Awareness. Bring it to their attention in a nonthreatening fashion: "I notice that you're . . ." "I know it's hard, but try to stay focused on what we are doing."

Identification and Sorting Out of Feelings. Help them to identify and sort out feelings. Help them understand that each person has a variety of feelings. Assure them that they won't be punished or rejected for their thoughts and feelings (James, 1989). See Chapter 4 for a discussion of feelings.

Conclusion

Many traumatized children behave in ways that can cause problems for themselves and discipline problems for us in the classroom. Often they react to everyday events in a way that may make no sense to the casual observer (Donovan & McIntyre, 1990). Only by understanding their behavior in the context of their lives can we make sense of it and learn how to deal with it.

Summary of Main Points

❖ Labeling students can blind us to appropriate discipline solutions.

❖ Misbehavior and underachievement can be reactions to childhood trauma.

❖ Identifying and labeling feelings is a vital skill for all children but especially for child victims of trauma.

❖ Traumatized children benefit from structure, routines, positive empowerment, and empathic attention.

Conclusion

Teaching is one of the most rewarding yet challenging professions. Caring Teacher's Discipline is designed to reduce the stress of teaching and to enrich the lives of both teachers and students. As caring teachers, we must not forget to take care of ourselves. Teaching is an extremely demanding profession—mentally, physically, and psychically. Collaborating with our colleagues, accessing community resources, and finding outlets, such as exercise and hobbies, can help reduce the pressures placed on us. The caretaker needs care also.

Caring Teacher Discipline helps children become good thinkers and learners as well as good classroom citizens. Caring teachers add three more "R's" to the traditional three "R's" of reading, 'riting, and 'rithmetic—respect, responsibility, and relationship. In doing so, we can indeed make a difference in the lives of our students as well as in our society.

> There is no beginning too small.
>
> —Henry David Thoreau

Resource A

Suggested Readings

Communication

Faber, A., Mazlish, E., & Nyberg, L. (1995). *How to talk so kids can learn at home and in school.* New York: Simon & Schuster.

Ginott, H. (1993). *Teacher and child: A book for parents and teachers.* New York: Collier.

Conflict Resolution

Crary, E. (1984). *Kids can cooperate: A practical guide to teaching problem solving.* Seattle, WA: Parenting Press.

Drew, N. (1987). *Learning the skills of peacemaking: An activity guide for elementary-age children on communicating, cooperating, and resolving conflict.* Rolling Hills Estates, CA: Jalmar.

Kreidler, W. J. (1990). *Elementary perspectives: Teaching concepts of peace and conflict.* Cambridge, MA: Educators for Social Responsibility.

Kreidler, W. J. (1994). *Teaching conflict resolution through children's literature.* New York: Scholastic Professional Books.

Kreidler, W. J., & Furlong, L. (1996). *Adventures in peacemaking: A conflict resolution activity guide for school-age programs.* Cambridge, MA: Educators for Social Responsibility.

Levin, D. E. (1994). *Teaching young children in violent times: Building a peaceable classroom.* Cambridge, MA: Educators for Social Responsibility.

Cooperative Learning

Johnson, D. W. (1994). *Learning together and alone: Cooperative, competitive, and individualistic learning.* Needham Heights, MA: Allyn & Bacon.

Saphier, J. (1987). *The skillful teacher: Building your teaching skills.* Carlisle, MA: Research for Better Teaching.

Sharan, S. (1994). *Handbook of cooperative learning methods.* Westport, CT: Greenwood.

Creating a Caring Community

Delisle, D., & Delisle, J. (1996). *Growing good kids.* Minneapolis, MN: Free Spirit.

Gibbs, J. (1995). *Tribes: A new way of learning and being together.* Sausalito, CA: Center Source Systems.

Kohn, A. (1990). The ABC's of caring. *Teacher Magazine, 1,* 52-58.

Lewis, B. A. (1991). *The kid's guide to social action: How to solve the social problems you choose.* Minneapolis, MN: Free Spirit.

Lewis, B. A. (1995). *The kid's guide to service projects: Over 500 service ideas for young people who want to make a difference.* Minneapolis, MN: Free Spirit.

Stone, K., & Dillehunt, H. Q. (1978). *Self-science: The subject is me.* Santa Monica: Goodyear.

Self-Esteem

Brooks, R. (1991). *The self-esteem teacher.* Circle Pines, MN: American Guidance Service.

Coopersmith, S. (1967). *The antecedents to self-esteem.* San Francisco: Freeman.

Phelan, T. W. (1996). *Self-esteem resolutions in children.* Glen Ellyn, IL: Child Management.

Writing Workshop

Atwell, N. (1987). *In the middle: Writing, reading, and learning with adolescents.* Monclair, NJ: Boynton/Cook.

Calkins, L. M. (1991). *Living between the lines.* Portsmouth, NJ: Heinemann.

Resource B

Recommended Programs

Conflict Resolution

The Committee for Children
2203 Airport Way South
Suite 500
Seattle, WA 98134
(206) 343-1223

Educators for Social Responsibility
23 Garden Street
Cambridge, MA 02138
(617) 492-1764

The Grace Contrino Abrams
   Foundation
1900 Biscayne Boulevard
Miami, FL 33132
(305) 576-5075

National Center for Resolving
   Conflict Creatively Program
163 Third Avenue, Suite 103
New York, NY 10003
(212) 387-0225

Creating a Caring Community

The Child Development Project
Developmental Studies Center
2000 Embarcadero, Suite 305
Oakland, CA 94606
(800) 777-7270

The Collaborative for the
  Advancement of Social and
  Emotional Learning
The University of Illinois at Chicago
Department of Psychology
Mail Code 285
1007 West Harrison Street
Chicago, IL 60607-7137
(312) 413-1008; FAX (312) 355-0559
(This is a clearinghouse that lists
  social and emotional programs.)

Community of Caring
1325 "G" Street, NW
Washington, DC 20005-3104
(202) 393-1251

Improving Social Awareness—Social
  Problem Solving Project
Dr. Maurice J. Elias, Professor
Department of Psychology
Rutgers University
Livingston Campus
New Brunswick, NJ 08903-5062
(908) 445-2444 or (908) 445-2056
e-mail: melias@rci.rutgers.edu

The KIDS Consortium
214 Coyle Street
Portland, ME 04103
(207) 871-0302

New Haven Public Schools Social
  Development Program
Hillhouse High School
480 Sherman Parkway
New Haven, CT 06511
(203) 946-7443

Paths Curriculum Development
  Research and Programs
130 Nickerson Street
Seattle, WA 98109
(800) 736-2630

The School Development Project
Yale Child Study Center
53 College Street
New Haven, CT 06510
(203) 737-1020

Self-Science Curriculum
Nueva School
6565 Skyline Boulevard
Hillsborough, CA 94010
(415) 348-2272

References

Aber, J. L., & Allen, J. (1987). The effects of maltreatment on young children's socioemotional development: An attachment theory perspective. *Developmental Psychology, 23*(3), 406-414.

Aber, J. L., Allen, J., Carlson, V., & Cicchetti, D. (1989). The effects of maltreatment on development during early childhood: Recent studies and their theoretical, clinical, and policy implications. In D. Cicchetti & V. Carlson (Eds.), *Child maltreatment: Theory and research on the causes and consequences of child abuse and neglect* (pp. 579-619). New York: Cambridge University Press.

Amabile, T. (1989). *Growing up creative: Nurturing a lifetime of creativity.* New York: Crown.

Bandura, A. (1973). *Aggression: A social learning analysis.* Englewood Cliffs, NJ: Prentice Hall.

Bowlby, J. (1982). *Attachment and loss.* (Vol. 1). New York: Basic Books.

Boyer, E. (1983). *High school: A report of the Carnegie Foundation for the Advancement of Teaching.* New York: HarperCollins.

Bredekcamp, S. (1987). *Developmentally appropriate practice in early childhood program serving children birth through age 8.* Washington, DC: National Association for the Education of Young Children.

Briere, J. N. (1992). *Child abuse trauma.* Newbury Park: Sage.

Cicchetti, D. (1989). How research on child maltreatment has informed the study of child development: Perspectives from developmental psychopathology. In D. Cicchetti & V. Carlson (Eds.), *Child maltreatment:*

Theory and research on the causes and consequences of child abuse and neglect (pp. 377-431). New York: Cambridge University Press.

Cicchetti, D., & Barnett, D. (1991). Attachment organization in maltreated preschoolers. Special issue: Attachment and development psychopathology. *Development and Psychopathology, 3*(4), 397-411.

Crittendon, P. M. (1988). Relationships at risk. In J. Belsky & T. N. Nezworski (Eds.), *Clinical implications of attachment* (pp. 136-174). Hillsdale, NJ: Lawrence Erlbaum.

Deci, E. L., & Flaste, R. (1995). *Why we do what we do: The dynamics of personal autonomy.* New York: G. P. Putnam.

Donovan, D. M., & McIntyre, D. (1990). *Healing the hurt child: A developmental-contextual approach.* New York: Norton.

Egeland, B., & Stroufe, L. A. (1981). Developmental sequelae of maltreatment in infancy. In R. Rizley & D. Cicchetti (Eds.), *Developmental perspectives on child maltreatment* (pp. 77-92). San Francisco: Jossey-Bass.

Elias, M. J., & Clabby, J. F. (1992). *Building social problem-solving skills: Guidelines from a school based program.* San Francisco: Jossey-Bass.

Fisher, K. W., & Ayoub, C. (1993). Affective splitting and disassociation in normal and maltreated children: Developmental pathways for self in relationships. In D. Cicchetti & S. L. Toth (Eds.), *Disorders and dysfunctions of the self* (Vol. 5, pp. 149-223). University of Rochester Press.

Garbarino, J., Dubrow, N., Kostelny, K., & Pardo, C. (1992). *Children in danger: Coping with the consequences of community violence.* San Francisco: Jossey-Bass.

Garmezy, N. (1984). Children vulnerable to major mental disorders: Risk and protective factors. In L. Grinspoon (Ed.), *Psychiatric update* (Vol. 3, pp. 91-104, 159-161). Washington, DC: American Psychiatric Press.

Gilligan, C. (1993). *In a different voice: Psychological theory and women's development.* Cambridge, MA: Harvard University Press.

Goleman, D. (1995). *Emotional intelligence.* New York: Bantam.

Gootman, M. E. (1995). *The loving parent's guide to discipline.* New York: Berkley.

Gordon, T. (1989). *Teaching children self-discipline at home and at school.* New York: Times.

Green, A. H. (1985). Children traumatized by physical abuse. In S. Eth & R. S. Pynoos (Eds.), *Post-traumatic stress disorder in children* (pp. 133-154). Washington, DC: American Psychiatric Press.

Greenberg, M. T., & Kusche, C. A. (1993). *Promoting social and emotional development in deaf children: The PATHS project.* Seattle: University of Washington Press.

Herman, J. L. (1992). *Trauma and recovery.* New York: Basic Books.

Hoffman, M. L. (1984). Empathy, social cognition, and moral action. In W. Kurtines & J. Gerwitz (Eds.), *Moral behavior and development: Advances in theory, research, and applications* (pp. 275-301). New York: Wiley.

Howes, C. (1990, April). *Social relationships with adults and peers within childcare and families*. Paper presented at the biennial meeting of the Society for Research in Child Development, Kansas City, MO.

Howes, C., & Hamilton, C. E. (1992). Children's relationships with caregivers: Mothers and childcare teachers. *Child Development, 63*, 859-866.

James, B. (1989). *Treating traumatized children: New insights and creative interventions*. Lexington, MA: Lexington Books.

Kardiner, A. (1941). *The traumatic neurosis of war*. New York: P. Hoebe.

Knitzer, J. (1990). *At the schoolhouse door: An examination of programs and policies for children with behavioral and emotional problems*. New York: Bank Street College of Education.

Kohn, A. (1991). Caring kids: The role of the school. *Phi Delta Kappan, 72*(7), 496-506.

Kohn, A. (1993). *Punished by rewards: The trouble with gold stars, incentive plans, A's, praise and other bribes*. New York: Houghton Mifflin.

LeDoux, J. (1989). Indelibility of subcortical emotional memories. *Journal of Cognitive Neuroscience, 1*(3), 238-243.

Levine, M. (1994). *Educational care*. Cambridge, MA: Educators Publishing Service.

Levinson, H. (1992). *Feedback to subordinates: Addendum to Levinson Letter*. Waltham, MA: Levinson Institute.

Lewis, B. (1991). *The kid's guide to social action*. Minneapolis, MN: Free Spirit.

Lewis, B. (1995). *The kid's guide to service projects: Over 500 service ideas for young people who want to make a difference*. Minneapolis, MN: Free Spirit.

Lewis, D. O., & Balla, D. (1976). *Delinquency and psychopathology*. New York: Grune & Stratton.

Lewis, D. O., Shanok, S. S., Pincus, J. H., & Glaser, G. H. (1980). Violent juvenile delinquents: Psychiatric, neurological, psychological, and abuse factors. *Annual Progress in Child Psychiatry and Child Development*, 591-603.

Lochman, J., Dunn, S. E., & Klimes-Dougan, B. (1993). An intervention and consultation model from a social cognitive perspective: A description of the anger coping program. *School Psychology Review, 22*(3), 458-471.

Lynch, M., & Cicchetti, D. (1992). Maltreated children's reports of relatedness to their teachers. In R. Pianta (Ed.), *Beyond the parent: the role of other adults in children's lives* (pp. 81-108). San Francisco: Jossey-Bass.

Maslow, A. H. (1982). *Toward a psychology of being*. New York: Van Nostrand Reinhold.

Masten, A., & Garmezy, N. (1985). Risk, vulnerability, and protective factors in developmental psychopathology. In B. B. Lahey & A. E. Kazdin (Eds.), *Advances in clinical child psychology* (Vol. 8, pp. 1-52). New York: Plenum.

Miller, A. (1990). *Banished knowledge*. New York: Doubleday.

Morrow, G. (1987). *The compassionate school: A practical guide to educating abused and traumatized children*. Englewood Cliffs, NJ: Prentice Hall.

Murphy, L. B. (1987). Further reflections on resilience. In E. J. Anthony & B. Cohler (Eds.), *The invulnerable child* (pp. 84-105). New York: Guilford.

Nelsen, J., Lott, L. L., & Glenn, H. S. (1993). *Positive discipline in the classroom: How to effectively use class meetings and other positive discipline*. Rocklin, CA: Prima.

Newby, T. J. (1991). Classroom motivation strategies for first-year teachers. *Journal of Educational Psychology, 83*, 195-200.

Oldfather, P. (1993). What students say about motivating experiences in a whole language classroom. *The Reading Teacher, 46*(8), 672-681.

Oppenheim, D., Sagi, A., & Lamb, M. E. (1988). Infant-adult attachments in the kibbutz and their relation to socioemotional development 4 years later. *Developmental Psychology, 24*, 427-433.

Ounstead, C., Oppenheimer, R., & Lindsay, J. (1974). Aspects of bonding failure: The psychopathology and psychotherapeutic treatment of families of battered children. *Developmental Child Neurology, 16*, 447-456.

Pederson, E., Faucher, T. A., & Eaton, W. W. (1978). A new perspective on the effects of first grade teachers on children's subsequent adult status. *Harvard Educational Review, 48*, 1-31.

Polansky, N. A., Chalmers, M. A., Buttenwieser, E., & Williams, D. P. (1981). *Damaged parents: Anatomy of child neglect*. Chicago: University of Chicago Press.

Polowy, M. (1992, April). *Effective management of angry, hostile, aggressive children*. Paper presented at the eighth annual training symposium of the Georgia Council on Child Abuse, Atlanta, GA.

Post-traumatic stress: Part I. (1991). *Harvard Mental Health Letter, 7*(8), 1-4.

Prothrow-Stith, D., & Weissman, M. (1991). *Deadly consequences: How violence is destroying our teenage population and a plan to begin solving the problem*. New York: Harper & Row.

Rachman, S. (1979). The concept of required helpfulness. *Behavior, Research, and Therapy, 17*(1), 1-6.

Redl, F. (1969). Adolescents: Just how do they react? In G. Caplan & S. Labovici (Eds.), *Adolescence: Psychosocial perspectives* (pp. 79-99). New York: Basic Books.

Reidy, T. J. (1977). The aggressive characteristics of abused and neglected children. *Journal of Clinical Psychology, 33*(4), 1140-1145.

Rockefeller, S. C. (1991). *John Dewey: Religious faith and democratic human-ism.* New York: Columbia University Press.

Rutter, M. (1987). Continuities and discontinuities from infancy. In J. Osofsky (Ed.), *Handbook of infant development* (pp. 1256-1296). New York: Wiley.

Rutter, M. (1990). Psychosocial resilience and protective mechanisms. In J. Rolf, A. Masten, D. Cicchetti, K. Neuchterlein, & S. Weintraub (Eds.), *Risk and protective factors in the development of psychopathology* (pp. 184-214). New York: Cambridge University Press.

Salovey, P., & Mayer, J. D. (1989-1990). Emotional intelligence. *Imagination, Cognition, and Personality, 9*(3), 185-211.

Sandberg, D. N. (1987). *Chronic acting-out students and child abuse: A handbook for intervention.* Lexington, MA: Lexington Books.

Schneider-Rosen, K., Braunwald, K., Carlson, V., & Cicchetti, D. (1985). Current perspectives on attachment theory: Illustration from the study of maltreated infants. *Monographs of the Society for Research in Child Development, 50*(5), 1-2.

Seligman, M. E. (1995). *The optimistic child.* Boston: Houghton Mifflin.

Silverstein, S. (1974). *Where the sidewalk ends.* New York: Harper & Row.

Silverstein, S. (1981). *A light in the attic.* New York: Harper & Row.

Snyder, C. R., Harris, C., Anderson, J. R., & Holleran, S. A. (1991). The will and the ways: Development and validation of an individual differences measure of hope. *Journal of Personality and Social Psychology, 60*(4), 579-585.

Spivack, G., Platt, J., & Shure, M. B. (1976). *The problem-solving approach to adjustment: A guide to research and intervention.* San Francisco: Jossey-Bass.

Spivack, G., & Shure, M. B. (1975). *Maternal childrearing and interpersonal cognitive problem-solving ability of 4-year-olds.* Paper presented at the annual meeting of the Society for Research in Child Development, Denver, CO.

Sternberg, R. (1990). Prototypes of competence and incompetence. In R. J. Sternberg & J. Kolligan (Eds.), *Competence considered* (pp. 117-147). New Haven, CT: Yale University Press.

Stone, K. F., & Dillehunt, H. Q. (1978). *Self science: The subject is me.* Santa Monica, CA: Goodyear.

Terr, L. C. (1990). *Too scared to cry.* New York: Harper & Row.

Terr, L. C. (1991). Childhood traumas: An outline and overview. *American Journal of Psychiatry, 148*(1), 10-20.

Thornton, S. (1995). *Children solving problems.* Cambridge, MA: Harvard University Press.

Tice, D., & Baumeister, R. (1993). Controlling anger: Self-induced emotion change. In D. M. Wegner & J. W. Pennebaker (Eds.), *Handbook of mental control* (pp. 393-410). Englewood Cliffs, NJ: Prentice Hall.

van der Kolk, B. A. (1987). *Psychological trauma.* Washington, DC: American Psychiatric Press.

Vygotsky, L. S. (1986). *Thought and language.* Cambridge: MIT Press. (Original work published 1962)

Werner, E. E. (1990). Protective factors and individual resilience. In S. J. Meisels & J. P. Shonkoff (Eds.), *Handbook of early childhood intervention* (p. 109). Cambridge, UK: Cambridge University Press.

Werner, E. E., & Smith, R. S. (1992). *Overcoming the odds: High risk children from birth to adulthood.* Ithaca, NY: Cornell University Press.

Wolfgang, C. H., & Glickman, C. D. (1980). *Solving discipline problems, strategies for the classroom teacher* (2nd ed.). Boston: Allyn & Bacon.

Zillman, D. (1993). Mental control of angry aggression. In D. M. Wegner & J. W. Pennebaker (Eds.), *Handbook of mental control* (pp. 370-393). Englewood Cliffs, NJ: Prentice Hall.

Zimrin, H. (1986). A profile of survival. *Child Abuse and Neglect, 10,* 339-349.

Index

CORWIN
PRESS

The Corwin Press logo—a raven striding across an open book—represents the happy union of courage and learning. We are a professional-level publisher of books and journals for K–12 educators, and we are committed to creating and providing resources that embody these qualities. Corwin's motto is "Success for All Learners."